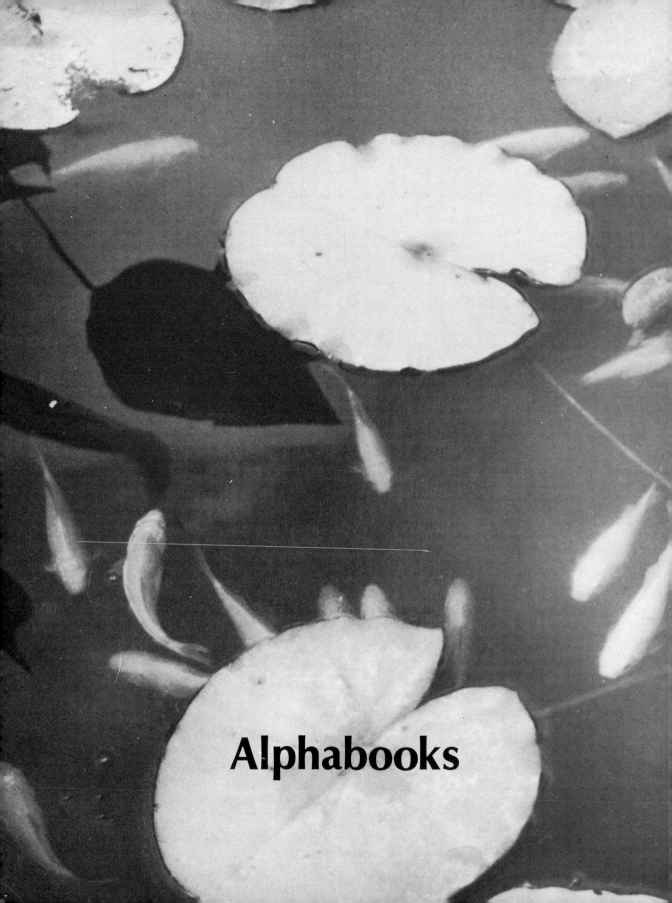

Alphabooks

Water Gardens

Gordon T. Ledbetter

Copyright © 1979 by Gordon T. Ledbetter

This book was designed and produced by Alphabet and Image, Sherborne, Dorset, England

First published in England in 1979 by Alphabooks, Sherborne, Dorset, England

Picture credits

The author and publisher thank the following for permission to use their photographs in this book: Alphabet and Image Library page 57; Heather Angel 40 (top left), 43 (top left), 46, 49 (bottom), 51 (right), 78 (bottom), 103 (bottom left), 104 (top), 107 (top), 111 (both), 112, 113 (bottom), 120, 126 (top), 128 (both), 129 (top); Edward Ashpole 122; Pat Brindley 11 (both), 12 (top), 41 (top right), 56 (bottom), 72 (both), 75; Natural History Photographic Agency 39 (top left), 40 (top right), 42 (bottom); John Parkhurst 43 (top right), 53 (bottom), 64 (and front cover), 69 (top), 71 (left); Laurence Perkins 104 (bottom), 106, 107 (centre and bottom); P. Scully 58 (bottom); Harry Smith Horticultural Photographic Collection 6—7, 13, 52, 53 (top), 54—5, 56 (top), 62 (bottom), 73 (top), 81 (bottom), 83, 84, 100 (right); Roy Pearce 43 (bottom left), 113 (top), 118—9, 129 (bottom); John Topham Library 2—3, 20, 32, 117; Michael Warren 68 (top), 77 (and back cover), 102. The remaining photographs are by the author. All line drawings are by Elizabeth Winson.

ISBN 0 9506171 4 8

Printed and bound by Butler & Tanner Ltd, Frome, Somerset, England

CONTENTS

page

Acknowledgments   6

1 Making a garden pond   7

2 Designing a pond   19

3 The secret of clear water   37

4 The water-lily   46

5 Marginal plants for the pool   65

6 Virtues and vices of a bog garden   87

7 Fish and livestock for the pool   105

8 Keeping a winter aquarium   115

9 Pitfalls, problems and pond care   122

10 Diary of a water garden   133

Appendixes   145

Index   151

Acknowledgments

In writing this book I drew upon the advice and expertise of many people. I should like to express my thanks to the Director of the National Botanic Gardens, Dublin, Aidan Brady, and his staff. In particular, Donal Synnott and Ann Hart who were so generous with their time and from whom I learnt so much, also Barney Brown and Denis McNalley.

To Rosemary ffolliott I owe a special debt of thanks for having allowed me to photograph one of her ponds during the course of construction, and for many kindnesses. To Niamh and Padraig Cusack who participated in the making of the pond and in the photography with such spirit, I am truly grateful.

For so patiently answering my incessant questions, I wish to thank Jim Ryan; and also, Dr Michael McKillan and Dr James O'Connor. Thanks are also due to: Anthony and Wendy Berry, Ann Chambers, June Jackson, Barney Johnson, Dolly Kempton, Joanne Kinsella, Edward Manning, Fred Nutty, David Proger, Eddie O'Connor, Bill Quigley and Carlos Rotas for their kind help.

To those who allowed me to photograph their splendid gardens I should like to express my gratitude. In particular I should like to mention: Mr and Mrs Patrick Annesley (Anne's Grove); Mr and Mrs R. A. Childers (Glendalough House); P. Colbert; Marty O'Gara; P. P. Manning; The Earl of Meath (Kilruddery); Roy Seymour; Mr and Mrs Slazenger (Powerscourt Gardens); and Mr Robert A. Walpole (Mount Usher).

I acknowledge with thanks the help provided by The Commissioners of Public Works; Marlfield Nurseries; Perry's Hardy Plant Farm Ltd; R. H. S., Wisley; and Wildwood's Water Gardens Ltd.

Finally, I should like to thank my sister, Audrey Baker, for much help and advice during the preparation of the text.

G.T.L., Co. Wicklow, Ireland

1 MAKING A GARDEN POND

A music critic once remarked of one of the great sopranos of long ago (Amelita Galli-Curci), that her voice always reminded him of 'water-lilies floating on water'. What the critic had in mind, of course, was an effortless, unblemished beauty, serene and chaste. It is what has made sopranos and water-lilies revered down the ages.

Water-lilies, however, differ from most *prima donnas* in one important respect. They do not require cossetting, are by no means temperamental. In fact, water-lilies are extremely easy to grow, as are many water-loving plants. And for the newcomer to gardening, a garden pool probably offers more certain and more rapid results than any other form of gardening. Once the initial work is completed, a pond involves less maintenance than, say, the equivalent area in grass, and much less work than a herbaceous border. Moreover, a pond can occupy a tiny space where a herbaceous border would look out of place or awkward. On the other hand, a pond can be made the centrepiece of the most ambitious combination of rockery and stone and brickwork. No other form of gardening has such wide appeal. No child can resist rushing to the pond's edge to watch the fish and glimpse the creepy crawlies. There can be few adults, even those normally indifferent to garden plants, who will not respond to the beauty of the water-lily. And even the nongardener is likely to find afternoon tea or an aperitif, taken by the pond, somehow tastes different. There is perhaps only one drawback to a water garden; and that, to be sure, is a serious one. It is simply not true that it takes half a metre of water to make a hazard for a small child. Even a puddle is a potential danger to any child who cannot swim, and that fact should never be forgotten. But that said, probably no other kind of garden is more likely to appeal to all your family; to become, indeed, a family institution.

Tub ponds

A taste for water gardening need not be an expensive one. Long gone are the days when a wealthy landowner would take it into his head to install a pond of solid lead; but one of the oldest forms of containers is still among the cheapest. Half a wooden wine barrel will make an excellent tub pond. Standing on a patio about waist high, a tub pond makes an attractive ornament in its own right. Sunk in the ground, the pressure of water within and that of the earth without will keep the wooden staves of the barrel holding water long after the metal rims have rusted away. A sunken pond is not as susceptible to changes in air temperature as a raised one, a feature for which water-lilies tend to be grateful. And there are miniature water-lilies which are well suited to the small surface area contained in a barrel. The limited growth of these plants means that their leaves will not flop helplessly over the sides. An old china sink would do as well as a barrel — indeed any container which is at least 30 cm. deep and which holds water will serve as a tub pond.

Prefabricated ponds

Next in convenience, though a great deal more expensive, is the modern prefabricated fibreglass or plastic pond. These are usually

A tub pond. Support the baskets containing the marginal plants with bricks.

designed with ledges upon which can be placed baskets to contain marginal plants. Digging out the site to conform to the irregular shapes of most prefab ponds requires a little more skill and care than does a perfectly round barrel or a rectangular pond. Dig out the site as closely as possible to the shape of the pond, at the same time removing any

An informal, plastic moulded pond complete with three ledges suitable for marginals.

sharp stones. The base and sides should then be given a surface of damp peat or sand. Upon this the prefabricated pond is bedded down and it is then immediately ready for filling. A disadvantage of prefab pools lies in their limited size; and more than that, the fact that you cannot choose or design the shape yourself which is surely half the fun.

Pool liners

No such drawback exists with what are called pool liners. These are largely made of plastics such as polythene; PVC (polyvinyl chloride); PVC laminated with a nylon weave; and Butyl rubber. PVC, whether it is reinforced or not, and Butyl rubber have the advantage of being stretchable. But all the materials are flexible and will snugly fit any shape. Too many abrupt contours and narrow inlets should, nevertheless, be avoided as it means overlapping the liner rather excessively. Besides, too many nooks and crannies, and small bays make a pond look fussy. Before cutting a single sod, map out the circumference of the pond you have in mind using a length of rope. (You might begin by putting your plan down on paper.) Remove the grass sods or the first few centimetres of soil within the area of the rope and you then have a blueprint of your pond. Any final modifications should be carried out at this stage. There is no difficulty about cutting out additional space in the pond later. But banking up crumbling soil to fill an unwanted corner or to make a promontory is much more trouble than leaving firm, well-packed soil where it stands. The same applies to ledges. When digging out the site, where you want ledges leave 30 cm. or more of bank between the rope and the excavation. Then remove soil from the bank to a depth of about 20 to 25 cm. Finally, all sharp or flinty stones must be scrupulously removed from the site before installing the liner. By adding a few centimetres of sand — easily applied when

Begin your pond by mapping out the circumference with a length of rope. View the result from every conceivable angle; make sure you have sufficient room all round the pond and make any necessary adjustments. Use an edge cutter and a spade to cut and lift the turves.

Making a garden pond

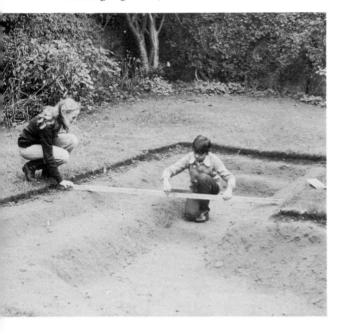

Once you have excavated the site, make sure that the banks are level all round. This is a tedious job but one worth taking time over. Incidentally, if you want to test that your level is in working order, place it on a straight piece of wood as in the picture to obtain a level reading. Then reverse it and if the bubble stays between the two marks then your level is giving correct readings. The shelf running the length of the left-hand bank and the bank at the far end will be used later to support marginal plants grown in baskets.

With the site fully prepared, the liner can be unfolded. In this case it is a PVC liner. If the day is warm, there is no harm in allowing the fully opened liner to lie in the sun for a few hours. This will add to its flexibility.

BELOW Lay the liner across the site and keep in place with bricks. You will find this job much easier to carry out if you choose a calm day.

damp — to the base and sides, it will be possible to stand in the finished pool without fear of damaging it — provided you wear soft-soled shoes. Similarly, heavy ornaments, if their bases are quite smooth, can be left to stand on liners quite safely.

Irrespective of how many ledges and contours are contained in your final layout, the dimensions of stretchable liners can be calculated in the following way. The length of the liner will consist of the maximum length of the pond plus twice the maximum depth. The width of the liner will consist of the maximum width plus twice the maximum depth. For example, a pond 2.4 x 1.9 x 0.9 metres deep, would need a stretchable liner 4.2 x 3.7 metres. If it is a non-stretchable liner you are installing, then the measurements must be taken more painstakingly. Run a tape measure from one bank over the ledges across the length of the base and up the bank at the far side. Do the same across the width. To both of these measurements add about 60 cm. so that the liner can be held in place under paving stones or rocks around the edge of the pond.

Removing stones from the site and making a marginal shelf. BELOW *A liner is held in place with planks; the rising water forces it against the sides of the site.*

To install a stretchable liner, simply lay it across the site with bricks holding it around the sides. Then direct a hose pipe into the centre of the pool and watch the weight of water carry the liner down to the base and cling smoothly to every contour around the sides with the minimum of wrinkling. As necessary, you can aid the process by allowing the liner to slide gently from under some bricks and pulling it up further under others. In cold weather the elastic quality of the liner may be reduced. This problem can be solved by leaving it in a warm room for some hours, if you wish near, but not in contact with, a radiator. To install a non-stretchable liner, lay it in the site and smooth it over the contours, slowly adding water all the time. Once the pond is full of water, the edges of the liner can be trimmed and held in place permanently by a layer of concrete or paving stones.

LEFT *Securing the liner in place with paving elements.*

BELOW LEFT *Trim the edge of the liner after the pond has been filled.* BELOW *When cementing the surround in place – in this instance bricks are being used – try to keep the liner taut as you lay the cement. Use a level when laying the bricks.*

While PVC and Butyl rubber are about five times as expensive as polythene, their life expectancy is much greater. Even the heavier grades of polythene are not to be recommended for permanency. Quite apart from what may happen to the polythene below water level, the area above the water line will be subject to the ultra-violet rays of the sun and these quickly make polythene brittle. The other kinds of liners are nothing like so vulnerable to the sun's rays and they last many, many years. Liners are available in various colours. Grey, often called 'stone', and black are the least conspicuous and so are the most natural colours. Blue, especially light blue, should be avoided, as it clashes badly with plants. And upon all underwater surfaces algae will adhere and grow, and blue shows up this growth. Some liners may be more algae-resistant than others, manufacturers at least claim as much, but it is only a question of degree. Sheets of Butyl rubber and PVC are normally sold in standard sizes. But these sheets can be vulcanized or welded together by the manufacturer as required. So virtually any size or shape of pond can be accommodated. It is also possible to tape sheets of liner together yourself, but the welding process is to be preferred. Puncturing is the worst problem associated with pool liners. However, repair kits are available for Butyl rubber and PVC. Polythene cannot be repaired satisfactorily.

Concrete ponds

Cracking is the main danger concerning concrete ponds. The unyielding strength of concrete is both its virtue and vice. Should the sides or base of a concrete pond be placed under greater stress than they can endure, the result is inevitably a crack. And even if that crack be no more than a hairline one, there is no certainty about the repair. Large cracks will be even more troublesome. A concrete pond may be the most durable of all, but this is only so if it is built to the highest standards in the first place. Compromise on the preparation of site, in the thickness of the concrete, omit reinforcement in the concrete, fail to allow for the expansion of water into ice, and disaster may well follow.

To begin with, satisfy yourself that the site is firm and stable. If in doubt thoroughly bed into the base and sides a layer of coarse aggregate (gravel). In an informal pond the sides should be cut so as to slope outwards at an

A fine example of a concrete pool. Note how the paving elements slightly overhang the bank.

The walls of concrete ponds are far less vulnerable to the pressure of ice if they are not perfectly upright. Aim for a slope of about 20° off the perpendicular.

angle of 20° or more off the perpendicular. This will reduce the pressure exerted on the concrete when ice forms. If the sides have to be perfectly vertical, as is usual with formal schemes, then the sides should be made as thick as the base. That is to say not less than 15 cm. thick. Sloping walls need to be at least 12 cm. thick, and it is important to avoid one very common mistake: do not allow the cement to slide down and bulge at the bottom of the wall so that it is thinner at the top. The concrete should be mixed in the proportions: one part of cement by volume to two of sand and three of aggregate. The aggregate should be composed of either gravel or crushed stone varying in size between 5 mm. and 20 mm. Use only materials supplied by a building merchant; should the sand or gravel contain any organic matter, such as decaying leaves, the strength of the concrete will be impaired and may even become porous. The addition of a waterproofing agent will not only improve the impermeability of the concrete but will add to its durability. Do mix the materials *dry,* and mix them all thoroughly. Then, and only then, add water. Failure to observe this procedure may result in the materials never being properly mixed. Add no more water than is necessary to obtain a consistency whereby it is possible to slice the concrete with a spade without the two sides becoming completely united again. Standard

reinforcing steel mesh or heavy gauge chicken-wire — and steel rods if it is a really large pond — should be used to reinforce the concrete. Care must be taken to ensure that the concrete penetrates the spaces between the wire meshes without leaving innumerable air spaces like a sponge. Rust is no problem, but wire which for any reason has been painted is unsuitable, and leaves or grass which have become enmeshed in chicken-wire must be thoroughly removed, or the wire rejected.

Formal ponds with perpendicular sides will need what is known as 'shuttering' to keep the concrete in place while it hardens. Shuttering consists of a frame (with easily removable sides) made of wood, chipboard or even hardboard and designed to fit into the pit leaving a gap the whole way round of 15 cm. Soapy water lathered on to the bank side of the shuttering will help to prevent the wood adhering to the concrete.

Concrete begins setting immediately it becomes wet. It stiffens noticeably after about twenty minutes in warm weather, and more rapidly in hot. The process can be slowed down by continually turning the mix over. It is as well to dampen the interior of the site. This will prevent the concrete losing moisture too rapidly once it is in place, which would have the effect of reducing its ultimate strength. Begin by laying down about 6 cm. of

Making a garden pond

RIGHT *Shuttering for a formal pond. It must be rigid but easily dismantled.*

BELOW *The well-defined border of this rectangular pond helps to define the area of water from the surrounding grass. Without so strong a border the pond would be far less conspicuous.*

concrete over the base. Place the reinforcement over this and then add concrete to make up the final thickness of 15 cm. Make sure that the wire mesh is completely smothered in the concrete without protruding at any point, except around the banks where it will be used to reinforce the sides. In the case of an informal pond, it should be possible to concrete the base and sides in one single operation. With small, formal ponds you may be able to put the shuttering in place while the base is still soft and so proceed immediately with the sides. (It really depends upon the weight of the shuttering and whether it can be installed without the necessity of walking on the base.) If you cannot put the shuttering in straight away, key or roughen the edges of the base to make a good joint with the sides later. Allow the base to harden, install the shuttering and add the walls. Old concrete will not bond with new, so the sooner the walls are added the better — I would certainly not leave the adding of the walls for weeks on end. Also, the earth banks will tend to crumble to some extent and it is imperative that you do not get soil mixed with the concrete at any stage. The fact, incidentally, that you have dampened the walls should help. And if the weather is very hot it is as well to lay wet sacks over the concrete while it hardens. The more slowly it loses moisture the better the concrete. Indeed it is worth filling the pond with water after twenty-four hours.

Calculate the amount of concrete you need by adding the surface area of the four walls to the area of the base and multiplying that figure by the thickness you intend making the concrete. For example, if you were making a pond 5 m. x 4 m. x 0.9 m. internal depth with the base and walls 15cm. thick, the calculations would be made as follows:

$$2 (5 \times 0.9) = 9 \text{ sq. metres}$$

(the two longer walls)

$$2 (3.7 \times 0.9) = 6.66 \text{ sq. metres}$$

(the two shorter walls)
i.e. each length less 2 x 0.15 cm. which is the thickness of the longer walls

$$5 \times 4 = 20 \text{ sq. metres} \quad \text{(the base)}$$

The total surface area therefore amounts to approximately 36 sq. metres. Multiply by the thickness: $36 \times 0.15 = 5.4$ cubic metres, which is the amount of concrete the pond requires. Ready-mix concrete becomes economical for any size of load above 3 cubic metres. And one would be well advised to have so large a load as 5.4 cubic metres supplied by a ready-mix company provided, of course, that the lorry can approach the site. Failing that, look into the possibility of hiring a small, portable cement mixer. In this case add half the coarse aggregate and half the water first, then add the sand. Once they are mixed, add the cement and finally the remainder of the coarse aggregate and enough water to produce the necessary consistency.

If you are buying the materials to mix yourself, then they should be calculated as follows. The ratio of the mix is 1 cement : 2 sand : 3 aggregate, that is to say there are 6 parts to the whole. Therefore, in 5.4 cubic metres one part will consist of $5.4 \div 6 = 0.9$ cubic metres. So one needs:

0.9 cubic metres of cement
1.8 cubic metres of sand
2.7 cubic metres of coarse aggregate

You may find that the builder's merchant supplies the materials not according to cubic capacity but according to weight. Unfortunately, there is no fixed ratio between the weight and cubic capacity of either sand or coarse aggregate. The ratio varies according to the character of the materials. It is better to use the density of concrete as a unit of measurement. (This is not absolutely accurate, but it is quite sufficient for pond building.)

The density of concrete can be set at 2.45 metric tons per cubic metre. So for 5.4 cubic metres the weight would be 13.23 metric tons. The materials can now be calculated as follows:

CEMENT: $\dfrac{13.23}{6}$ = 2.205 tons

Each bag of cement weighs 50 kilos, so 45 (44.1) bags are required.

SAND: $\dfrac{13.23}{6}$ x 2 = 4.41 (say 5 tons)

AGGREGATE: $\dfrac{13.23}{6}$ x 3 = 6.615 (say 7 tons)

It is always safer to slightly overestimate your needs to allow for wastage. Remember that the number of joints should be kept to a minimum. Try to complete the pond in no more than two operations.

If you live in an area with very severe winters, you can make a concrete pond of great strength by employing a technique more usually used for swimming pools. It consists of building a double wall of concrete blocks and filling the gap between the two walls with solid concrete. Steel rods can be inserted in the blocks as they are laid and this will provide massive strength. The blocks will not be waterproof, they simply provide the strength. It is the concrete between the two walls that makes the pond watertight and it must be very thoroughly compacted. An important point to note is that when laying the blocks, surplus mortar must not be allowed to collect on the base between the two walls. If it does, the inner concrete wall may not make a watertight joint with the base.

This is an expensive method of pond building and a time-consuming one. As against that, it does mean shuttering is avoided and this is worth bearing in mind where large-scale, geometric designs are concerned.

Whereas with fibreglass and liner ponds it is usually possible to make some adjustment to the level of the walls after the pond is completed, with concrete structures it is never possible. Nothing looks worse than water halfway up one bank and brimming over the other. Building up the offending wall is useless as the bond will not be watertight. So it is worth taking the trouble to level the site before carrying out the concreting. Use a straight board and a level. If the site is too large to stretch the board from one bank to the other, drive a stake into the centre of the base so that it is level with the lowest bank. Then remove the surplus soil from the other banks, taking readings with the board and level as you go.

Alkali will leach out into the water from new concrete, and this is harmful to both plants and fish. It can be prevented by painting the interior surfaces of the new pond with a sealing agent. Alternatively, the new pond can be 'cured' by filling and emptying it of water several times over a period of some weeks. The addition of enough permanganate of potash to colour the water purple, or

A pond wall of massive strength. Solid, instead of hollow concrete blocks can be used, and the reinforcing rods omitted without serious loss of strength.

17

Cross-section of a pond showing how planting depths can be arranged.

acetic acid, will speed up the process. Apart from the curing process, you may want to empty the pond from time to time. The old idea was to dig out a pit, fill it with cinders or rubble, and run a pipe from it to the pond. In very porous soils, it was sometimes suggested that no more than an outlet pipe — perhaps composed of the top half of a bottle with a rubber stopper — would be sufficient. None of these ideas is to be recommended, for several reasons. Apart from the additional work involved in digging out another pit, if the outlet pipe becomes clogged it will be almost impossible to clear it. And above all, if the joint between concrete and pipe is not perfect or leaks later — what if you crack the top of the bottle? — it cannot be rectified. It is a far more satisfactory practice to use an electric pump.

Finally, you are bound to have mused over how deep to make your pond. Deep ponds are more attractive than shallow ones, but the main consideration is the depth of water that various water-lilies like over their crown (see Chapter 4). Generally speaking, if one allows a depth of 20-30 cm. for the soil and 45-70 cm. for the water above the soil, that is sufficient. In other words a total depth of between 65 and 100 cm. Only so far as large water schemes are concerned is it worth increasing the depth above one metre.

These then are the available means of making a garden pond. Having decided upon the materials you wish to use, the next stage is to consider design possibilities.

2   DESIGNING A POND

A well made patio pond in a front garden. Raising it by just a few centimetres has added a great deal to its attractiveness.

A good landscape gardener and a good photographer have much in common. Just as a good photographer knows exactly how to compose his shot before taking it, so a good landscape gardener should have a clear idea of what he wants before starting work on the site. Considerable experience is required in order to visualize precisely how any particular design may look in practice. Few amateur gardeners — and by no means all professionals — can accurately conceive a project entirely on paper or in their heads. Most gardeners will modify their initial scheme as it progresses. Nevertheless, the more clearly you can visualize and plan your water garden in advance the more satisfactory will be the result.

You should begin by deciding which type of water scheme best suits your needs: a patio water garden; a formal pond with or without other forms of gardening and with or without fountains and waterfalls, or an informal pond with or without embellishments.

The patio pond

If you live in an inner city environment with no more than a small but sunny patch of ground for a garden, then a patio water garden might well be the answer. A tatty patch of lawn with one or two meagre shrubs can hardly be regarded as a garden at all; but a

19

A formal Mediterranean water garden. The layout is admirable but has sufficient space been left for walking around the corners of the pond?

patio and pool can, and with no more maintenance, indeed less, than that required of a lawn of the same area. Moreover, a pond, no matter how small, is a legitimate focal point in a way that a rose bush is not. If you doubt this, consider the suggestion: 'Let's have lunch round the rose bush.' Nothing sounds more odd, and nothing more natural than: 'Let's have lunch round the pond.' Countless thousands of backyards, too small and ugly for conventional gardening, could be transformed by making them into patio water gardens. If you are a person who is away from home for long periods, who only sees the garden at weekends, who likes neither weeding nor mowing the lawn, a patio water garden offers the ideal solution. The same is true if you happen to be the fortunate owner of a *pied-à-terre* away in the country or in some foreign land. A patio water garden can still look fresh and attractive after long periods of neglect. Finally, a patio and pond offer opportunities to anyone who owns a roof garden, which is usually limited to potted shrubs.

For the owner of a large garden, a patio pond is likely to be regarded as no more than an optional extra. No one would want to convert a whole area of rolling lawns and well laid out borders into paving stones and water. The most popular idea in such cases is to combine the patio with the back wall of the house, the pond perhaps being visible from the house through French windows (but not so close to the windows that one steps straight out of the house into the pond!). Wherever the patio is situated, so far as a large garden is concerned, it should be combined with some other feature of the garden — if not the back of the house, then a hedge or a wall (p. 77). A

20

patio, alone, in the middle of a garden of any size will look stark and out of place.

Patio ponds are usually formal in design. A formal, regular shape nearly always harmonizes best with the strong, clear shapes of paving stones or bricks. But a pond should never be square. For some strange reason, a square always appears dull, even deadening (which presumably accounts for that piece of American slang: 'He's a square'). Make your pool rectangular; and if you have sufficient space, you might have one large rectangle bordered at each corner by a smaller one. Or the pond might consist of two interlocking rectangles. There is no limit to the number of geometric designs one can envisage. But do not make the pond too complicated or fussy. One soon becomes irritated with a fussy design. And above all, do not make your pond so broad or long that you cannot walk the whole way round it with plenty of space to spare. Quite apart from the fact that every

This little pond neatly fills an empty corner. In Britain the walls might create too much shade, but on Menorca there is no problem.

A split-level patio pond with iris beds

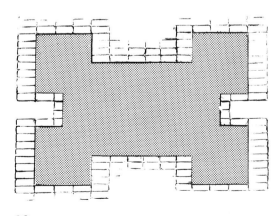

A variety of possible pond shapes.

visitor under the age of eleven will be certain to fall into the pond or make a good attempt at doing so, you want to give the patio a sense of spaciousness. The patio should never appear to have been squeezed in, as an afterthought, between the pond and the surrounding wall. The smaller the patio, the smaller should be the pond in proportion to it. Rarely should the length and width of the pond exceed one third of the length and width of the patio.

This is even more important if you decide upon a raised pond. If your space is limited, a raised pond will tend to make the area appear even more confined. On the other hand, if your patio is surrounded by wrought iron work or a light railing, as is the case with many roof and terrace gardens, a raised pond will help create a welcome sense of solidity. And it does have the advantage of bringing the plants and livestock closer to view. (Having a broad coping stone on the wall makes an excellent seat.) Flexible liners can be used for raised ponds just as well as concrete. The liner simply needs to be held in place by being cemented between the last line of bricks and the coping stone.

When levelling the patio area it will also be necessary to take into account the thickness of the paving units. To do this, mark the thickness of the unit on the ends of a series of wooden pegs. Drive one of the pegs into the ground so that the top of it is flush with the earth surrounding the patio area. The ground should then be whittled away until the mark appears. Using a straight board and a level, the remaining pegs can be driven in at intervals so that they are level with the first. The soil is then removed to the depth of the mark on all the pegs. Finally, remove the pegs and again check on the level of the ground.

If you are using paving units which are regular in shape, then the length and width of the patio and of the pond must be multiples of the measurements of one such unit. For example, let us say that one paving slab measures 75 x 90 cm. Then the width of the pond should be a multiple of 75, and the length a multiple of 90. For example, if it were planned that two paving slabs should match the length and width of the pond, then the pond

An outstanding example of a formal patio pond on Roman lines, designed by H. A. Peto (1854–1933), on the island of Ilnaculin (Garinish), Co. Cork, Ireland.

Levelling a site by means of pegs and a level

would have to measure 2 x 75 cm. by 2 x 90 cm. i.e. 1.5 x 1.8 metres. On the basis that the patio should not be less than three times as long and as wide as the pond, it must measure at least 4.5 x 5.4 metres. So for this patio 32 paving slabs are required: (24.3 — 2.7) ÷ 0.675 (i.e. the total area of the patio minus the area for the pond, divided by the area of one paving unit).

When a large number of small paving units is involved, it may be necessary to take into account the width of the joints, and modify the dimensions of the pond accordingly. However, this is not usually necessary with small patios as the width of the joints can be taken up by a slight overhang of the units immediately surrounding the pond. (To standardize the width of the joints, a couple of wooden pegs — about 13 mm. thick — can be placed temporarily between the units.)

There is little difficulty about using large paving slabs. But laying down a complicated pattern needs a great deal of forethought and measurements have to be exactly right. And it becomes more difficult when the paving units are of more than one kind or colour. There is a useful moral in the cartoon of the little man laying down black and white tiles in a baronial hall. He comes to the last space and then discovers that whether it be a black or white tile that he puts down, he is going to have two tiles of the same colour side by side. It is not a bad idea to lay out the pattern before excavating the pond. This way you can be certain that the dimensions of the pond fit the pattern.

Concrete slabs can be safely laid on sand, or set in mortar. The slabs round the pond, no matter how immovable they may seem, are best set in mortar. Make sure the earth is very firmly tamped down before laying the slabs, and add coarse aggregate if necessary. Small

LEFT *A lovely combination of water, lilies, ferns and large paving elements. Again note how the elements overhang the pond by several centimetres.*

ABOVE *A superb example of brickwork. The curving steps heighten the sense of the pond being the central feature.*

paving elements, such as cobbles, tiles and bricks should be set in mortar. It is often more satisfactory to prepare a solid concrete foundation 50-60 mm. thick, prior to bedding down the paving elements on mortar. Due allowance must be made for the depth of the paving element, the mortar and concrete foundation. And if the patio is bordered by a lawn, sink the paving elements by an additional 15 mm. in order to facilitate cutting of the grass. The mortar can be made by mixing one part of cement with three of sand. Be sparing with the water. Spread the mortar to a thickness of about 25 mm. (50 mm. in the case of sand), lay down the paving stone and lightly tap into position. Any mortar that gets on the surface of the paving slabs should be wiped off immediately to prevent staining. The joints can be filled later with mortar or sand, depending upon which you have used for the foundation. You might find a dry-mix mortar speeds up this operation. Fill the joints with the cement and sand mix, then,

very lightly, add the water. The risk of staining the patio is reduced with this method.

Irregular stone is by far the easiest kind of paving to lay. The only point to remember is that all the large pieces should not be clumped together in one part of the patio and all the smaller ones in another. This can happen if you do not start off with the firm idea of mixing all sizes together. If you want an informal pond, then 'crazy paving' or irregular stone is the obvious material to use, and will look well in almost any scheme.

Glazed tiles and to a lesser extent smooth-faced bricks will tend to give your patio garden an atmosphere of coolness. In warm climates this may be exactly what you want. In more temperate zones, the same tiles may create a sense of coldness rather than coolness. And glazed tiles, while attractive in themselves, give the impression of being slippery, which indeed they may be, especially when wet. Remember too that tiles have to be laid on a very smooth and firm foundation; any bumps or

25

3 sizes of paving unit

bricks

2 sizes of paving unit

crazy paving

2 sizes of paving unit

bricks or paving units of same size

A variety of paving patterns

aberrations are very obvious in a tiled patio. Embossed tiles or bricks which have been given a slightly roughened appearance in production — often called rustic bricks — help create a warmer and I think more welcoming environment. Bricks are adaptable and look well in any size of garden, although there is a great deal of work involved in laying them.

Concrete slabs are available in all sorts of shapes and sizes, and square, rectangular, octagonal and hexagonal slabs are all popular. And they can be laid quickly and easily. Their bold and individual outlines may, however, come across as too strong and marked in a small garden. Match the size of your paving elements to the size of your garden: the larger your patio, the larger can be the elements. If you have a soil foundation, then spaces can be left in the patio in which to plant shrubs or trees. Where space permits (you do not want to cast too many shadows over the water), four of those marvellously thin, slender and compact *scopulorum* Junipers could be planted at the four corners of a formal patio pool. They will provide a great depth to the garden by their reflection in the water.

Raised beds offer another, and greatly underrated, possibility. The walls of the beds could be made from a contrasting material; the patio might be made of concrete and the beds of brick, or one might use two different tones of concrete. A different tile, brick or whatever, might be used as a surround to the pond to highlight it as the central feature. Contrasting colours can, of course, be used as 'veins' in the pattern of the patio, but without an experienced eye such attempts may turn out woefully fussy and over done. Simplicity is no sin.

Informal ponds

And simplicity is certainly no sin in the design of a formal pond. For it is precisely by its broad sweeps and well defined lines that a formal water scheme makes its appeal. And the same applies to informal ponds. Here one is not aiming at geometric clarity; but a natural water scheme is quite different from a chaotic one, and it is achieved by simple, well-laid out plantings and groupings of plants. The question is when to opt for a formal pond and when an informal one. Personal taste is likely to be the first consideration, but the layout of your garden as it already exists needs to be taken into consideration. By and large, a highly formalized garden with trees, shrubs and hedges laid out with geometric precision, demands a pond of equal precision. As a general rule the lines of the pond should conform with the lines of the adjacent hedges or walls. The overall geometric layouts must be one of harmony. Strong lines that do not run parallel or are not laid out at very definite angles will look awful.

That said, geometric and formal lines are more easily destroyed than created. Should you inherit a formal garden and wish to alter it, nothing could be easier. The severity of a hedge can be softened by the planting of shrubs at various places along its length. A

Kilruddery: a formal pond with cut granite coping over brick walls. The cost of granite stone and the work of a skilled stonemason sadly makes the cost prohibitive for most purposes today.

geometric border can be made into an informal one, simply by cutting out curved sections along its edge. An informal pond, if combined with a rockery, is not so likely to clash with an otherwise formal garden. If you create a rockery, make sure the rocks or boulders you use are buried in the soil to at least half their height, preferably more. You might think it a waste of rock and effort to conceal it. But a rock simply stuck on top of the soil looks very unnatural.

Waterfalls

A rockery opens up the possibility of including a waterfall, which can be made in a number of ways. Fibreglass 'saucers' are obtainable and these are simply sunk into the rockery, so that water falls from one saucer into the next without any water spattering on to the surrounding soil, otherwise the level of the pond will drop. Simple as fibreglass saucers are to install, they hardly ever look as natural as those made of concrete. If your concrete saucers are light enough to lift, it is an advantage to make them away from the site and put them in place later. Dig out shallow moulds in some spare ground and line with polythene or straw. Prepare the cement as you would for making a pond, using less aggregate if you wish. A stiff mix is essential. Place in the moulds and smooth to the required shape, having thoroughly embedded chicken-wire as reinforcement. Then at one end form a 'lip' about 10 cm. across. This can be made with a long, flat piece of stone if desired; but it is important that the lip is several centimetres below the level of the surrounding wall, or as water builds up in the saucer it will cascade

over the sides as well as the lip. The depth of the saucers need not be equal, but to prevent water spilling over, they should not be too shallow. An average waterfall needs 15 to 30 cm. Once the concrete is hard the saucer can be bedded into position in the rockery. The advantage of making the saucers off site lies in being able to angle them later to obtain the best pour. On the other hand, when making large waterfalls the cascades must be constructed in precisely the right position as they cannot easily be adjusted afterwards. But you can combine the saucers or cascades with rocks (they would be too heavy to move into position from a mould). Make absolutely certain, however, that all rocks and stones embedded in the concrete do not reappear

ABOVE *A series of cascades on site.* LEFT *A close-up of a typical concrete cascade. Note how the cascade is 'lipped' (using, in this instance, a flat stone), and how the cascade below is sited well under the fall of water.*

A very fine example of a man-made waterfall, one of a series in a large natural water scheme at Glendalough House.

cult to lay out satisfactorily. The inevitable creases and overlaps in the liner are hard to conceal and it is by no means easy to prevent the surrounding soil from continually entering the water course.

Waterfalls and courses can be fed by one of two kinds of pumps. What are known as submersible pumps will provide an output of anything from 1000 to 4,500 litres of water per hour, with a head of water of about a metre (the vertical height of the highest cascade above the water level of the pond). As the water head is doubled, the output can be expected to be reduced by about one third. The bore, length and any bends in the outlet pipe will also have a bearing on the output. Usually the pump manufacturer will state the output at various heights, indicating the maximum head possible for that particular model. Up to 1000 litres per hour will provide a gentle tinkling waterfall, while 4,500 litres will be closer to a torrent. For most purposes 2 - 3000 litres per hour is quite sufficient.

The pump is simply submerged in the pond so that the chamber of the pump (which contains a centrifugal impeller) is automatically filled with water. The outlet pipe is then

A typical waterproof pump that can be placed on the bottom of the pond. The electric cable is connected to the mains supply via a transformer.

underneath. If they do, the likelihood is that water will seep out between the concrete and rocks. A waterfall will look more natural if it begins some way up the rockery rather than at the top.

A water course, where the water runs between rocks and boulders, can be constructed in conjuction with, or instead of, a waterfall. The procedure is the same. Dig out a channel in the rockery and line with concrete and rocks or small boulders. The sides of the channel must be of sufficient height to avoid water spilling over, a special danger where curves are encountered. Water courses can be made from liner material but they are diffi-

The overhanging maple creates so much shade that lilies can be grown only in one corner.

to be housed in a weatherproof and ventilated container adjacent to the pond. A factor known as 'suction lift' has to be taken into account; that is to say the pump must not be more than a certain height above the water level of the pond. But this is rarely a problem, as the suction lift factor (provided with each pump) is not likely to be less than 1.3 metres. An intake pipe is fitted with a strainer and foot-valve (to prevent water pouring back out of the pump when it is not in use). The outlet pipe is put into the top cascade and the system is

directed from the pump up to the top cascade, it being concealed in the rockery soil and by a plant or rock where it enters the cascade. The pump should be connected to an electrical point installed near the pond by a qualified electrician. (Water and electricity can make a lethal combination, so it is best not to try such an installation oneself.) By using a T-piece in the outlet pipe, a waterfall and fountain can be fed from the one pump; and by inserting stopcocks in the two outlet pipes it will be possible to vary the output between the waterfall and fountain.

Surface pumps, as they are called, are much more trouble to install than submersible ones and are generally more expensive. But they do have an advantage in that their performance is affected less by the length or height of the outlet pipe; and where a huge display of fountains and cascades is required, surface pumps can provide the output — 15,000 litres per hour if necessary. The surface pump has filled with water: the pump is primed. Perhaps the easiest way to prime the system is to first remove the foot-valve, inject water from a hose pipe into the outlet pipe and then start the pump. The pump cannot draw up water when the impeller chamber is empty and to run the pump when dry may lead to overheating and damage. Once the water is circulating, the valve can be replaced. Then the pump can be stopped and started as required.

To protect the pump from weeds and debris, a corner of the pond can be walled off with fine wire mesh, for example, and the intake pipe placed within.

Water in motion raises the oxygen level in a pond, so fish will appreciate a fountain or waterfall. Water-lilies, unfortunately, will not. They like neither being continually dowsed in water — the flowers will tend to close up and sink — nor do they like disturbed water. So far as a fountain is concerned, unless your pond is large enough to accommodate one in one area and the lilies in another, they make poor companions. Besides, fountains are really only appropriate in formal schemes.

The case against waterfalls has, I think, been overstated. Not only will a waterfall raise the oxygen content but by moving the water through oxygenating plants, it will filter from the water the fine particles of mud held in suspension. Large baskets of *Elodea* will answer this need very effectively. Place them so that they are directly in line with the current of water. To maximize the filtering function of the waterfall in relation to underwater plants, I would place the intake pipe at the *opposite* end of the pool to the waterfall. I know that many gardeners would frown at

31

such a practice. Place the intake pipe under the waterfall and minimize water disturbance, is the usual advice. But a reasonable compromise between the needs of the lilies and the filtering process is usually possible, since you are hardly likely to want to run the pump continuously, and where there is no perceptible current, the lilies will hardly notice. A more sophisticated but also more troublesome method of filtering water is possible. A box of fine sand, fitted with a retaining gauze exit and entrance is connected up to the outflow pipe (the intake pipe must never be interfered with). The sand will need to be changed at the end of every season. Properly installed, this is a very efficient method of filtering, but it can be a messy business getting it right. And a point to remember is that the output of the pump will be reduced.

Bridges

A bridge can add as much to a garden pond as a waterfall. The pond needs to be designed so that it narrows at some point, preferably somewhere near the middle, and there the bridge can be spanned. If the pond is of much the same width throughout, a bridge may look out of place. Probably the easiest kind of bridge to make is a wooden one. Two strong beams are placed side by side to span the channel. They can be secured by burying in the soil or in concrete. Planks are then cut and screwed into the beams at right angles. The width of a bridge should be at least 60 cm. for convenience. A concrete bridge is almost as simple. Make a wooden 'trough' — which

This bridge shows a high standard of craftsmanship. Much of its elegance derives from being so slender. Its strength depends on its graceful curve.

can be easily dismantled — and lay it across the channel. Fill with concrete and reinforcement. The sides and top surface can easily be faced with stones or paving slabs. The thickness of the bridge will depend upon its length and the weight it must carry.

An arched bridge requires a great deal more effort and skill. For this, one has to build an arched frame made of wood. Plywood bent over a series of formers is probably the simplest method of making such a frame. This must span the channel precisely and just come in contact with two concrete foundations set in the soil on either side. The foundations should be slightly lower than the soil so that they are not visible. The concrete for the arch will need to be made fairly firm, otherwise when you lay it on the wooden frame it will part in the middle and slump down on either side. The value of the foundations is that they will act as a buffer to the

60 cm.

1.5 m. span   10 cm.

For foot traffic over curved or flat concrete bridges these figures represent the minimum reinforcement and thickness of concrete required.

3 m. span   10 cm.

It is important, to avoid cracking, that the bars are embedded in the lower third of the concrete and this must be well compacted. At the same time ensure that there is 25 mm. or more of concrete below each bar.

bars 10 mm. thick

A simple form of bridge: a solid piece of granite. Its cost would not be related to its simplicity and it would take several men to put it in place.

wooden frame

concrete foundation

keystone

surface brick facing

concrete

gap cut in frame for keystone

frame pulled out to support facing bricks

Method of constructing an arched bridge comprising of concrete and bricks. Considerable skill is needed to produce a workmanlike result.

bridge as it sets. It would not be impossible, however, to construct the bridge without them. Simply dig out the soil on either side of the pond to receive the bridge and do the concreting in one job. Work is made much easier if the curve of the arch is not too great. It also means the bridge will be easier to walk over. A concrete arched bridge can be very effectively faced with bricks. One course of bricks is laid cross-wise over the top of the concrete form. Two further courses are arranged in 'fan shape' on either face of the bridge. (The inclusion of a larger key-stone adds a tremendous amount to the appearance of a bridge, if you can get one made.) Once the concrete part of the bridge is quite hard, you can face its top surface and then carry out the fan work as follows. Take off the side of the frame which was used to hold in the wet concrete. Move out the wooden frame on one side of the bridge to the width of one brick. The bricks can then be supported by the frame until the whole arch is completed, when it becomes self supporting. If a large keystone is being used, you may have to cut out a space in the wooden frame to accommodate its

greater length. Having done one side, the frame can then be pushed through the bridge to appear on the other side, and the second set of bricks is cemented in place. To start this 'fan work' it is important to have two concrete foundations finished *at such an angle* that the fan of bricks can be started directly against them. A bridge of this kind does need a certain standard of craftsmanship. Any part of it which is not quite right will show up badly. But such a bridge offers great opportunities for individual touches of design and the results can be very satisfying.

Cost

How much might a pond cost? Like almost any building project, there is no ceiling to what one can pay. But water gardening can certainly be regarded as an inexpensive pastime. An attractive, moderate-sized pond is within the reach of anyone. I would suggest, however, that you avoid the cheaper types of liner. Using polythene is false economy. If you do decide on a liner pond, it is only wise to buy the best, that is the heavier grade of Butyl rubber or PVC with nylon laminate. All these liners cost much the same and their cost is similar to that of concrete (excluding the additional labour involved.) Fibreglass or plastic ponds run at about three times the price of concrete and liner ponds. Taken as an example, a modest sized pond, say 1.8 x 1.2 x 0.75 metres deep, would require a stretchable liner 3.3 x 2.7 metres or 0.76 cubic metres of concrete. There is no point in giving the actual monetary cost of such a pond, since inflation is likely to make nonsense of the figure within a short time. But one can give a comparative value. Such a medium-priced pond would cost roughly the same as a man's sports jacket. Adding a submersible pump would more or less double the price. The cost of liners rises in proportion to their increase in size. The price of pumps increases by between 50 and 75 per cent as their output doubles.

The addition of a patio would be your largest single cost. For the pond in question, one would need a patio at least 5.4 x 3.6 metres: 19.44 sq. metres. Pre-cast concrete slabs are

Stepping stones serve more than a decorative function; they can give access right to the centre of the pond, for planting and maintenance.

among the cheapest kinds of paving units. Using 60 cm. square slabs, one would need a total of 48 slabs, i.e. (19.44 - 2.16) ÷ 0.36. Roughly speaking, 50 concrete slabs would

ABOVE *A 'formal' waterfall is an excellent way of joining two split-level ponds of formal shape.* RIGHT *A devilish fountain mask gushing forth water in three jets. Wall fountains of this kind with a tiny pond beneath are a clever way of decorating a small area.*

35

cost about the same as the liner and pump combined. So as a guide to the cost of a small patio pond, one could say it would be the equivalent of two sports jackets and one medium-priced suit. Clothes vary in price of course. But this comparision indicates the sort of money one is talking about.

Your new pond, freshly filled with water, will have a crystal clarity. But as you will discover, that state will not last. Quickly or slowly, the water will discolour until it becomes a murky green. The process is inevitable. But no less inevitable is the process by which this state is reversed. Without changing the water, the original clarity can be regained permanently. Having built your pond, the next step is the judicious planting of underwater plants.

Kilruddery: an example of landscaping towards the end of the seventeenth century. This large pond is one of a pair; the water-lilies were added at a much later date.

3 THE SECRET OF CLEAR WATER

Water turns green because the mineral salts it contains, the sunlight it absorbs and the carbon dioxide given off by fish and pond animals, are just what the minute spores of green algae need to exist and multiply. When present in their millions, these tiny organisms clutter the water to such an extent that everything else in the pool is invisible. Changing the water is no more than a temporary solution because the process will immediately begin all over again, and in any case water-lilies require undisturbed water. The pond looks hopelessly polluted when vast amounts of algae are present, although, in fact,they are not harmful to fish who will happily feed off these organisms. Algae are simply unsightly.

The answer to clearing a pond of algae, or at least to radically reducing their number, is to starve them of their needs. Water weeds (or oxygenating plants, as aquarists call them) will fulfil this function. Actually to describe underwater plants as oxygenators is really only to describe half their function, and not necessarily the most important one. Oxygen is absorbed by water through surface contact with the surrounding air and plants add to that process. But they also absorb the carbon dioxide and mineral salts essential to algae. And once the oxygenating plants have appropriated all the available food, the algae, in the unequal struggle for survival, simply die, and the pond becomes crystal clear. Do bear in mind, however, that between filling the pond with water and the establishment of oxygenating plants, algae will thrive. A 'pea soup' period has to be endured in the confidence that if you have a sufficient number of oxygenating plants they will win in the end, and the algae will be reduced, as one writer so brightly put it: 'to a fine shower of corpses'.

And with only temporary lapses, the water should remain permanently clear. The lapses are most likely to occur in spring after a sudden spell of warm, sunny weather. The algae will immediately start into growth and conditions will be favourable to them. During the dormant winter period there will have been a build up of waste animal matter. The pond will be in a eutrophic or nutrient-rich condition. And this state will remain until the oxygenating plants are again growing actively. Then the pond will return to a comparatively oligotrophic or mineral-deficient condition and the water will clear. And it is surprising how quickly the change occurs. One day you may be glumly looking at the 'soup' and the next into water almost as transparent as a mountain stream.

It is impossible to say what amount of oxygenators any particular pond needs. The factors are far too complex and variable. They would include the amount of sunlight the pool receives, the depth and temperature of the water, its mineral and animal content and much more. But it can be said that all underwater plants will carry out the dual function of removing carbon dioxide and adding oxygen to the water. Their presence is absolutely essential to clear water. As a rule of thumb — and it is no more than that — if a third of the total volume of the pool appears to contain oxygenators, then that should be sufficient. But there is no reason why the pond should not contain more. The propagation of many oxygenators is very simple. All

that is required is to snip off the top few centimetres of a stem. Stick this in the soil and it will develop quite happily. Alternatively, a whole plant with its roots can be weighted down with a piece of lead and simply dropped into the pond to root naturally on the bottom. Strips cut from an empty tooth-paste tube make good weights. All underwater plants reproduce vegetatively and they can often be divided up after only a couple of months. Instead of laying down a layer of soil over the whole base of the pond, it is now common practice to grow plants in baskets. When the pond is made of concrete either way is possible. Liner pools require the use of baskets because stones contained in a layer of soil might puncture the liner when walked upon or when soil is being removed. Oxygenators grown in baskets will very soon creep over the sides and root themselves in any debris on the bottom. So when you want to reduce their number, all you have to do is remove the baskets, take out all the surplus weed in the bottom of the pond and then return the baskets. Most oxygenators will quickly take over a pond, so baskets are a useful way of keeping them in check.

Many ponds are oxygenated and purified by one or more of the Elodeas. The North American Water Thyme or Ditch Moss, *Elodea canadensis (Anacharis)* is an excellent purifier but also a most vigorous one especially outside its native habitat. It may have been recorded in Ireland in the 1830's and reached England in the early 1840's. But the most celebrated transference of the plant occurred in 1847-8, when the Curator of the Botanic Gardens at Cambridge, England, received specimens of the plant from a Professor Babington and placed them in a tributary of the River Cam. Within a few years the plant had monopolized huge stretches of the Cam, making swimming and boating all but impossible, and actually raising the level of the river. The weed became known as 'Babington's

Elodea canadensis – Canadian Pondweed or Ditch Moss

Curse'. Its prodigious ability to spread was carried out purely vegetatively, as only female strands of the plant had been imported. *E. canadensis* caused the same problem in other places where it was planted or transferred. Then after some years its vigour, for some reason, declined and the plant became a civil enough member of the plant community. When introduced to 'new' water it does seem to regain some of its lost vigour and may not settle down for some years. When I first used the plant I found my pond was very quickly taken over. Then after about five years its rate of reproduction seemed to slow down. If your pond is small enough to be swept clean of the surplus by hand, there is no real problem. The surplus makes a fine fertilizer.

For large ponds, you could use *Elodea densa (Egeria densa)* which is also an excellent oxygenator while being less prolific. The two plants are very similar in appearance and they are not easy to distinguish. The easiest way of identifying them is through their flowers. *Densa* throws up conspicuous three-petalled white flowers above the surface, whereas if *canadensis* flowers at all, it will have tiny pink or white flowers, floating on the surface on

the ends of long strands. The leaves of *canadensis* are produced in whorls of three or four and each leaf is usually minutely toothed. (You may need a magnifying lens to make out the teeth.) Leaves of *densa* are toothless or nearly so and produced in crowded whorls. And there are usually four leaves to each whorl. In a mature plant the leaves will be 2.5 cm. long at least, whereas the leaves of *canadensis* should be a great deal less than that. *Elodea callitrichoides* is larger than the other two, having leaves over 3 cm. long in whorls of three or occasionally two. *Elodea crispa (Lagarosiphon major)*, which has alternate leaves about 3 cm. long, is more suited to the aquarium than the outdoor pond as it is not fully hardy. Incidentally, when identifying these plants, bear in mind that considerable variation occurs from locality to locality. The length of leaves, for example, can vary greatly.

If you are collecting your underwater plants from the wild rather than from a stockist, wash them well before introducing into the pond if you have fry about. There may be parasites attached to the leaves. Adult fish

The small, three-petalled white flower of Elodea densa is the surest way of identifying it.

LEFT *Callitriche stagnalis – Water Starwort,* and ABOVE *Ceratophyllum demersum – Hornwort.*

will usually feed off any insects that come into the pond in this way. Many underwater plants are notoriously difficult to identify even for the trained botanist (and let it be said that classification of underwater plants is neither exhaustive nor always clear), but unless you have a huge pond in which rampant weeds are going to cause a problem, strict identification is not necessary. All plants that produce underwater leaves (as opposed to those whose leaves begin under water only to rise above it later on), will function as water purifiers. If you are collecting 'blind' however, concentrate on still water. Some oxygenators can adapt themselves to both running and still water, but others are only capable of surviving in one situation. And introduce several different species into your pond, not only for the sake of variety, but also because some species will probably do better than others under the conditions particular to your pond.

The Callitriches comprise a large genus that one is certain to find in the wild. The Common Water-Starwort, *Callitriche stagnalis,* is to be found throughout much of Europe. It is well suited to cold water but not to warm,

hence its absence from Mediterranean areas and from indoor aquariums. It has a preference for shallow water and will continue to grow during the winter — a useful feature. So too will the Autumnal Starwort, *C. autumnalis,* which, however, is not fussy about temperatures. It also has the advantage of not breaking the surface, a feature shared by the Hornworts, *Ceratophyllum demersum* and *submersum.* If you have a deep pool, *demersum* is a particularly good choice as it will fill whatever depth is provided for it. The Willow Moss, *Fontinalis antipyretica,* is another excellent oxygenator and a beautiful one into the bargain. It has long foliage, not unlike seaweed, but of a rich, vivid green. Obtain a whole plant with the roots intact if you can. It is more likely to be found in running water, attached to a rock or stone, than in still water. As the name *antipyretica* might imply, it is non-combustible and was once used as a form of fire insulation between chimneys and walls.

If you like the idea of including an oxygenator with attractive flowers held well above the surface, then one can hardly do better than to obtain the Water Violet, *Hottonia palustris,* which produces whorls of light purple or sometimes white flowers. In the American form, *Hottonia inflata,* the flowers are always white. The Water Violet is not always an easy plant to transfer. Featherfoil is another name for the plant, not to be confused with Parrot's Feather, which is the common name of *Myriophyllum prosperpinacoides.* One can hardly regard this lovely plant as an ideal oxygenator since it likes nothing better than to rise out of the water and, given the opportunity,

BELOW *The Water Violet, Hottonia palustris. The plant is not, in fact, related to the Violet but to the Primrose family. The name 'violet' comes from the colour of the flowers.*

Myriophyllum prosperpinacoides — Parrot's Feather

hang gracefully over the edge of a bank or side of an aquarium. It has been used on occasions in hanging baskets filled with water, so that the finely cut leaves and the gorgeous light green colour of the plant appears right before one's eyes. The lovely feathery foliage, as well as the colour, certainly justifies such treatment. And Parrot's Feather is well worth including in the pond for its ornamental value. It does need to be wintered indoors as it is not fully hardy. Spiked Water Milfoil, *Myriophyllum spicatum,* is quite hardy, has feathery foliage too and is common in many waterways in Europe. In summer it sends up very small but nonetheless conspicuous red and yellow flowers, which is an added bonus in a plant which is an excellent purifier. More widespread is *Myriophyllum verticillatum* which is found in North America and Australia as well as Europe. The plant is of similar appearance to the spiked form but the flowers are insignificant.

For a mass of white buttercup-shaped flowers floating or just raised above the surface, grow the Water Crowfoot or *Ranunculus aquatilis.* It is a common and very easy plant to find and it is a good example of how adaptable nature

One of the sub-species of Ranunculus aquatilis, the Water Crowfoot. It produces a mass of small but showy white flowers during the summer.

can be. The plant has two distinct kinds of leaves. Those under water are finely divided, which enables the functions of collecting carbon dioxide and giving off oxygen to be carried out efficiently. The leaves on the surface are not more than deeply lobed and are, of course, quite flat so that the leaves can float and maintain their equilibrium. A carpet of Water Crowfoot running the length of the bank is an attractive feature in spring when the flowers appear. If you want to use it as an oxygenator, plant it in reasonably deep water otherwise the underwater leaves may not develop. Two other plants are worth mentioning, for if you do not find them in the wild, you are sure to find them in an aquarist's shop. One is Tape Grass, *Vallisneria sprialis,* which bears long, twisting and strap-like leaves emerging from the base. It forms runners and so useful colonies of these plants develop in a tray or in soil laid on the bottom of the pool. The other, *Potamogeton crispus,* Curled Pondweed, has broad, buckled and crimped leaves of a bronze hue, which makes the plant distinctive in any pond.

So-called floating plants, those which for at least part of the year live on the surface of the pond, are not effective as oxygenators. But they do play a part in keeping the water clear in so far as they cut down the amount of sunlight the algae receive and by using some of the nutrients in the pond. They are primarily grown for their ornamental value. The Common Duckweed, *Lemna minor,* is a very familiar sight: those little bright green discs which cover many a wild pond and ditch. Fish may enjoy it, but it is rather prolific and if you introduce it into your pond, you may involve yourself in tiresome thinning-out operations. The same is true for all the Lemnas with one notable exception. That is *Lemna trisulca,* the Ivy-Leaved Duckweed. It consists of oval or elliptical fronds of a greeny transparency, and the fronds are linked together by thin strands. If you have experienced trouble in keeping your pond clear, get hold of this duckweed, it is excellent for purifying water. If you have seen the Fairy Moss, *Azolla caroliniana,* you are bound to have been struck by its delicate tones of green in summer and vivid red in autumn. It is, without doubt, a beautiful plant; but be warned, it is not simply

Vallisneria spiralis – Tape Grass

ABOVE *Hydrocharis morsus-ranae – Frogbit*

TOP *Lemna minor – Lesser Duckweed*
ABOVE *Azolla – Water Fern*

prolific but can take over a pond in the manner of a wall-to-wall carpet. So thorough is the Fairy Moss in covering the surface of a pool that it has been used in Panama and elsewhere to prevent mosquitoes laying their eggs in the water.

Rather like a miniature water-lily is Frogbit, *Hydrocharis morsus-ranae,* which has light green, round to kidney-shaped leaves not much larger than a thumb nail, and little white flowers. In winter the plant dies off but not before producing terminal buds which become separated from the parent plant to lie on the bottom of the pool until the following spring. Of similar habit is the Water Soldier, *Stratiotes aloides,* which only makes a brief appearance on the surface and looks like the top of a large pineapple. For most of the time the Water Soldier is submerged. Like the Frogbit, it produces side shoots or bulblets which lie dormant until the spring and the mature plants only appear to produce their white flowers. The plants then sink back again. *Stratiotes aloides* is calcareous, that is to say it prefers limestone waters. And this may explain why it does not always transfer readily. On the other hand, it can be prolific; but the plants are so large (30 cm. across) that they can easily be removed by hand as necessary.

If you are prepared to go to the trouble of wintering plants indoors, then you can try growing the most beautiful of all floating plants, the Water Hyacinth, *Eichhornia crassipes (speciosa)* — see p. 78. I say try because it really

A striking display of the Water Soldier, Stratiotes aloides.

needs plenty of warmth and sunshine to thrive and to flower. On the St John's River, Florida, the plant earned the title: 'the million dollar weed' on account of the way it obstructed navigation. Outside tropical and sub-tropical climates, it is, however, much less prolific. It floats by having a greatly inflated petiole or leaf stalk, which looks like a small green balloon perched on the water. Above the balloon,

A mature specimen of the Water Lettuce, Pistia stratiotes with two or three young plants appearing as side shoots.

the stalk narrows and then broadens into a fairly round and curled leaf. The entire plant is a shiny light green. It would be worth growing for that alone, but the flowers are quite superb, a light lilac blue with a spot of yellow, borne on spikes held high above the plant. The bushy, dangling roots, incidentally, make an excellent spawning ground for goldfish. Another plant worth growing for its foliage is the Water Lettuce, *Pistia stratiotes,* which indeed looks rather like a flat lettuce, one that has been gently sat upon. The leaves are a pale shade of green. This is not an easy plant to grow. It requires a temperature in excess of 20°C., and soft water; and it does better in shallow water with its roots within reach of soil. Finally, if you are lucky enough to be able to find them or obtain a few seeds of the Water Chestnut, *Trapa natans* (p. 78), a European native naturalized to a limited extent in North America, you can enjoy the fruits raw or roasted. They are sweeter before the shells have hardened. Apart from being edible, the plant is worth growing for its beautiful bronze and green foliage. It is an annual, the fruits rarely ripen in Britain and the plant appears to be growing scarcer on the European continent.

If you happen to live within easy reach of a

horticultural establishment which specializes in aquatic plants, do not let your enthusiasm run away with you. Can I make a plea for a stretch of plain water? In every pond, whatever the size, the reflection of waterside plants is one of the finest qualities that water can provide. Too many floating plants and oxygenators breaking the surface will spoil or destroy that quality. And besides, there should not be so many floating plants on the surface as to detract from the greatest of all aquatic plants: the water-lily.

A beautiful woodland pond at Glendalough House excavated in the middle of the last century when it was possible for a well-to-do landowner to call up fifty men for the job. Today the work would be done by machine. The island is an attractive feature and well worth including since there is still plenty of water surface. The scene would, I think, appear far less tranquil if most of the water was given over to water-lilies.

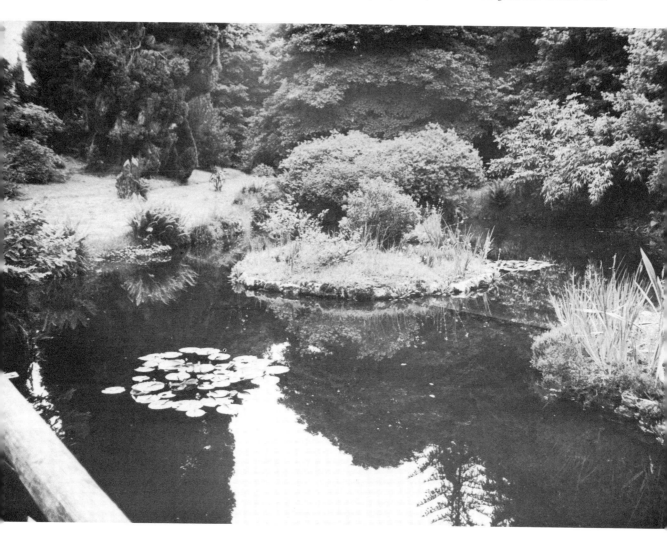

4

THE
WATER-LILY

The number of hardy water-lilies, hybrid or otherwise, runs into hundreds rather than thousands, as is the case with Rhododendrons, for example. The reason has less to do with the popularity of ponds than with the notorious difficulty of hybridizing the hardy species. Most of the hardy cultivars are infertile and cross-breeding of the few natural plants has hardly ever produced satisfactory results in any systematic way. The exceptions belong mainly to the work of M. Joseph Bory Latour-Marliac (1830-1911) of Temple-sur-Lot in the south of France. During the 1880's when pond building had become a high Victorian fashion, Marliac developed some method of crossing water-lilies. Some of his best hybrids bear the Latinized form of his name, *Marliacea,* or that of his son-in-law, Maurice Laydeker *(Laydekeri).* And without doubt, Marliac's hybrids are among the finest available. Sadly, his techniques died with him. He once said it would take forty years of hard work to re-discover them. So far no one has. And the temperate regions of the world are still waiting for a hardy blue water-lily.

Conceivably, we may not have to wait for a pure fluke. For there appears to be a revolution round the corner, not only as regards producing hybrids from water-lilies, but from the entire plant kingdom. That revolution would consist of the art or science — really a bit of both — whereby part of the recipe

(DNA) for one plant is spliced with part of the recipe of another. To produce a hardy blue water-lily, the object of the exercise would be to obtain the hardiness of, say, *Nymphaea alba* and combine it with the blue of the tender, tropical *Nymphaea caerula.* The problem is to identify and, more difficult, to select out the relevant ingredients for such a recipe. We may also look forward to a hardy lily which will remain open until dusk and perhaps on into the hours of darkness. A floodlit pool on a summer's evening can be a superb sight, but one which has the drawback of water-lily blooms which are invariably closed. Only among tropical lilies are there species which will open and flower at night.

A water-lily of average vigour can be expected to cover a surface area of about 1 square metre. One might nearly double that figure for the more vigorous varieties and halve it for the smaller and miniature forms. The surface spread will depend not only on the species but also on the depth of water, the richness of the soil and whether or not you are growing your lilies in containers. When given complete freedom as in a natural pond, or in a concrete one with soil spread over the entire base, a water-lily is likely to double its surface spread over about three seasons. The usual practice is to lift and divide the plants about every third year, otherwise the lily pads no longer float serenely over the water but clump up together. When buying your plants calculate to cover no more than a half to two thirds of the whole surface area of your pond. There is no reason why you should not cover a smaller area, except one plant placed in the corner of a large pond will look decidedly lonely. But the most common mistake is to have too many plants. The pond then looks cramped and your view of fish and underwater life becomes restricted. Do not underestimate the importance of large areas of water free of any plant or obstruction. A pond without that lacks one of its greatest attributes.

Laying down a layer of soil over the entire base is only practicable in a concrete pond. When it has to be renewed — a troublesome business at the best of times — it is risky scraping out soil and pebbles from a liner pond. Similarly, permanent brick containers are best used only in connection with concrete. There is much to be said for the now popular practice of using plastic containers. Thinning and dividing the plants is made much easier. You can also re-position plant and basket without having to lift the plant and set back its growth. And it is surprising how often one finds a reason for re-positioning water-lilies. There are lily baskets designed for the purpose: wider at the top than the bottom and with slits cut in the sides to allow the free passage of water. Until the roots have developed there is a tendency for soil to seep out of these slits. A simple remedy lies in lining the basket with hessian or any old rags. Most water-lilies require a basket about 30 x 30 x 20 cm. high, while a miniature plant would be satisfied with a container as small as 20 x 20 x 10 cm. I have seen lilies grown in plastic milk bottle crates which are sturdy but too large for comfort. Not for the comfort of the water-lily, which will happily fill all available space, but for the comfort and convenience of the pond owner. A lily plus soil and water in a container 30 cm. square

is quite heavy enough for anyone of average strength.

Water lilies are rich feeders, and yet I am continually surprised to find how well a plant will do in soil that is no more than 10 cm. deep and which has not been renewed in years. Ideally, however, lilies should be grown in rich, heavy loam such as one can obtain from the top spit of pasture. Cow manure that has been well matured under cover for several months can be added at the rate of about one part to three or four of loam — a spade-full to each basket. To prevent the manure fouling the water, it is a good idea to place a final layer of plain soil over the mixture; and a light sprinkling of gravel over that may reduce the amount of mud fish tend to produce by grubbing around in the baskets. Cow manure is optional; it can be omitted or crushed bonemeal can be used instead, but never add horse or hen manure which will pollute the water.

Hardy water-lilies belong to two genera: *Nymphaea* and *Nuphar*. Unless you happen to small pond, then choose the little *Nuphar pumila (minima)* which flowers freely, has very small leaves and is nothing like as vigorous as the other two.

The rootstocks or rhizomes of Nymphaeas are of two kinds: those which grow horizontally and those which tend to grow vertically or almost so. From the angle at which the leaves are emerging from the rootstock, it should be possible for you to judge which kind of plant you have. If in doubt, simply make sure that the crown of the plant is above the level of the soil when you plant it. Perhaps more water-lilies fail by being completely buried than for any other reason. The best time for obtaining plants is in late spring after growth is well under way. Water-lilies should not be moved before growth has started nor, for that matter, after growth has ceased in autumn. A young lily plant will be given the best possible chance if it is started in shallow water. Either place your plant and basket on a series of bricks and keep removing

LEFT *This lily was started in a plastic bag and is now being transferred to a larger basket. Heavy loam layered with well rotted cow manure and left under cover for six months or more is the ideal growing medium for water-lilies. But remember that cow manure that is not well matured is a boon to algae. Many gardeners prefer to use only loam and omit the manure.* ABOVE *Placing the basket and lily in the pond.*

have a stretch of water 1.8 metres in depth or more, or the water in your pond is very acid, then Nuphars are hardly worth growing. They will succeed under both these conditions whereas Nymphaeas will not. The common *Nuphar lutea*, known as the 'Brandy Bottle' on account of its faintly alcoholic smell, is to be found in many European canals, natural ponds and waterways. It has small and round yellow flowers, insignificant compared with any of the Nymphaeas. The North American *Nuphar advena* has slightly larger flowers which, like *lutea,* rise well clear of the surface. But since the leaves are always produced in abundance and measure about 30 cm. long, the flowers, which are only about 7 cm. across, are not very conspicuous. If, however, you do want to grow a *Nuphar* in a

Nuphar lutea – Brandy Bottle

49

ABOVE *An informal liner pond with a variety of water-lilies and marginal plants.*

gradually increase the depth of water over the plants. Replanting of the tubers into separate baskets can take place as soon as they each have a number of well-developed leaves.

Water-lilies are adaptable plants, but they should be chosen not only for their shape and colour but for the depth of water to which they are best suited. The most vigorous plants will thrive in depths of 0.75 to 1 metre and more. Plants of medium vigour are normally grown in depths ranging from 45 to 60 cm., while the small and miniature plants need no

bricks to lower the plant as it gains in vigour, or start with the pond only partially filled and gradually top it up. When you buy a water-lily plant you may get a tuber which has been cut off a parent rootstock. After a few seasons your young tuber will have matured and developed several offspring of its own. It is a simple matter to slice through the tubers, and the divided rootstocks can be replanted. If you want to propagate a large number of plants , lift the tuber and examine it for 'eyes'. These are small, immature buds, no more than little bulges, not unlike large warts with tiny leaves, growing on the tuber. These can be gouged out with a sharp knife, leaving a little of the main tuber on the 'eye'. Prepare a shallow tray of equal parts of sharp sand and loam, and a little crushed charcoal can be added to keep the soil sweet. Plant the 'eyes' in the tray, making sure that their crowns are exposed, and place the tray in very shallow water — 2-3 cm. is quite deep enough to start the eyes. Fish and stray bits of oxygenating plants should be kept well away from the tray. And a piece of net wire placed over the tray may discourage birds from rooting around in it and, as sometimes happens, pulling up the baby tubers. As leaves develop,

BELOW LEFT *A mature lily tuber. The long, white hairless roots are anchor roots and can be cut off before replanting the tuber, if desired. Roots with 'hairs' are those which provide the plant with nutrition and should be left intact.*

BELOW *A fairly well developed lily 'eye' or nodule. If gouged out this eye would quickly develop into a mature plant.*

BOTTOM *The tuber of a mature water-lily such as 'Gladstoniana' would be as thick as your arm. By comparison this young tuber of the miniature Nymphaea helvola is smaller than a thumb.*

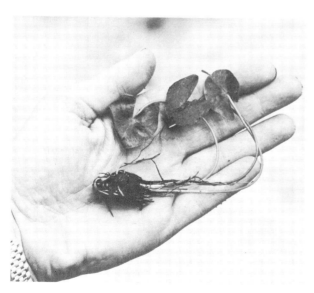

more than 20-30 cm. of water above their crowns. This, at least, is how commercial growers usually classify their plants. But, with the exception of the miniature water-lilies, one could certainly add at least another 25 cm. to the depth in each case and that would be, in my opinion, an advantage. You may wonder what happens if a lily is placed in a depth of water other than recommended. In water that is too deep, a plant may not have the stamina to send leaves to the surface and so it will eventually die; or it may survive but flower only occasionally or not at all. On the other hand, in water that is too shallow, the flowers will be small and not necessarily more numerous, the leaves will not be able to spread out properly and will quickly heap up

ABOVE *This lily plant is either too vigorous for the depth of water or it requires thinning back.*

on each other. Shallow water does have one advantage, however. It will warm up earlier in the season and the plants will develop and flower earlier. This might be worth bearing in mind if you live in northerly latitudes, Scotland or Norway for instance, which have short growing seasons, or if for some reason your pond is not exposed to direct sunlight throughout the day. Otherwise I recommend growing water-lilies in water which at least approaches the maximum rather than the minimum depth. The blooms will be larger, and the leaves, well spread out, will give the plant a much finer appearance.

If you have a large, deep pond or a lake and you want a white water-lily, then *Nymphaea* 'Gladstoniana' might well be your first choice. Under ideal conditions this very vigorous plant can produce massive white flowers 20 cm. across and more. It should be grown only in very deep water — 1.3 metres is not too deep — as it produces a great number of leaves. Slightly smaller and less vigorous, but no less beautiful, is the native European water-lily, *Nymphaea alba*. Many a wild lake is given a touch of serenity by the lovely white flowers of this plant. It will grow in slow moving rivers and is sometimes to be found in water as much as 3 metres deep. For the more moderate water scheme N. 'Marliacea Albida' is an excellent choice as it is a very prolific bloomer. Double flowers are not at all common among water-lilies, but Marliac's 'Gloire de Temple-sur-Lot' produces magnificent flowers, each containing a profusion of petals which makes this plant, unmistakably, a true double. The petals, at first, are tinged with pink and clear to white the day after the flowers open. 'Temple-sur-Lot' may take a few seasons before reaching its full blooming capacity. 'Gonnère' is another double, without quite the same density of petals, but a good choice, nevertheless, for the medium to deep pond. The North American *Nymphaea odorata* is a vigorous white water-lily suitable for ponds of medium depth, while the less vigorous 'Albatross' is better suited to the smaller pond. And if you have only a tiny tub pond or a sink, then choose the smallest white lily of all, *N. pygmaea alba* which has flowers 3.5 cm. across and needs only a few centimetres of water over its crown.

Most pond owners will want to grow more than one lily. To obtain the maximum contrast with a white lily one should choose a red

Nymphaea 'Escarboucle'

LEFT *Nymphaea 'Gladston-iana'*. BELOW *Nymphaea alba*

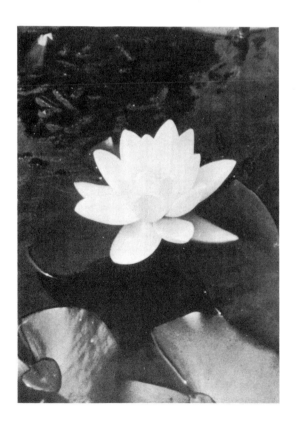

variety. By general consent the most outstanding red available is *Nymphaea* 'Escarboucle'. It produces large, deep crimson flowers which are probably the most conspicuous of any water-lily. 'Escarboucle', you may find, throws up red flowers blotched with white during its first season. The following year, however, the flowers will be perfectly red. The same sometimes applies to the offshoots. Do not think that your plant has some ailment, it is simply a characteristic of 'Escarboucle'. Medium to deep ponds are best suited to this lily. At the other end of the scale, for shallow ponds, *N.* 'Froebeli' (p.63) surely ranks as one of the best reds. In colour it is not unlike 'Escarboucle' since it has deep wine-red flowers. These rise well above the surface of the water and are produced in abundance. 'Froebeli' will flower well into the autumn, and I fancy will remain open in colder weather than most. In vigour mid-way between 'Escarboucle' and 'Froebeli' is *N.* 'Laydekeri Purpurata', another plant with rich red flowers and very free-blooming. If you are attracted to having both red and white in the same flower, then grow 'Attraction' which is of medium vigour and which produces garnet red flowers tipped with white. For deep water, there is 'Conqueror' whose flowers become a darker red from the centre outwards and are flecked with white. And for the large pond, one might well choose the magnificent 'Charles de Meurville' which sends up massive red flowers, but which needs plenty of space. More adaptable as regards depth is 'Gloriosa', whose blooms darken with age from carmine to deep rose. This is a plant which will thrive in water of medium depth but it will also do well in deeper water if necessary.

Sometimes described as a red lily is 'James Brydon' (p.63). Rich pink is, I think, a better description. This American lily is arguably the best choice of all to make if one were limited to a single specimen. In the first place the number of flowers the plant produces in relation to the number of leaves is high. The plant will continue to flower even when cloudy weather or reduction in sunshine prevents most others flowering. And the flowers of 'James Brydon' are very beautiful. Cup-shaped, exquisitely formed, with an even distribution of this rich pink hue — unobtainable in any other water-lily — it has vivid golden stamens which are well set off by this pink cup. And finally, 'James Brydon' makes a good cut flower. It requires a pool of shallow to medium depth. If this lily has a drawback, it lies, I think, in the very definiteness of that pink. Something more delicate is obtainable in the muted, blush pink of a 'Marliacea Carnea' or the denser pink of 'Marliacea Rosea'. Both plants have dark green leaves and are of medium vigour. For the larger, deeper pond 'Colossea', another blush pink and a prolific plant, would be a good choice. A double pink is to be had in 'Mme Wilfron Gonnère, not to be confused with the double white, 'Gonnère'. For star-shaped flowers held high above the surface, choose *N. odorata* 'W. B. Shaw' which is suitable for shallow to medium depths. So also is *N. tuberosa rosea*, which produces soft pink flowers, and like 'W. B. Shaw' is usually described as fragrant. But one normally has to approach a lily bloom closely before the fragrance is apparent; hardy water-lilies will not fill the air with sweet scent in the manner of a honeysuckle. For the smaller pond, 'Laydekeri lilacea' is a good choice, requiring only a limited amount of space. It has flowers that vary in colour from soft to deep rose. In the same bracket is 'Rose Arey', notable for its incurving petals.

If one is limited to two plants, I am inclined to think that a combination of a yellow with a white lily is preferable to either coupled with red. Red and pink are more dominant colours which demand attention. A soft yellow has a quiet grace which one may feel is more in keeping with the restful, soothing ambiance that one expects of a small garden pond. With this in mind, one could hardly do better than choose the almost impalpable yellow of 'Marliacea Chromatella'. This lovely plant is well suited to medium to deep ponds. The smaller, less vigorous 'Moorei' has flowers of a slightly darker yellow. Otherwise the plants are almost identical, their leaves being dark green, heavily blotched or spotted with purple. The large yellow flowers of 'Sunrise' make it a popular plant, especially as it is adaptable, vigorous in deep water but not uncontrollable in shallower depths. 'Colonel A.J. Walsh' is certainly a vigorous plant producing canary yellow blooms high above the water. It does tend however, to look rather unwieldy. Another plant which holds its blooms high is *N. odorata* 'Sulphurea Grandiflora'. It is nothing like so vigorous as 'Colonel A.J. Walsh', so it

Nymphaea Mme. 'Wilfron Gonnère'

55

LEFT *Nymphaea pygmaea alba*

BELOW LEFT *Nymphaea 'Sunrise'*. RIGHT *Tropical water-lily, Nymphaea colorata.*

should be grown in about 50 cm. of water. And a miniature yellow is available in *N. pygmaea* 'Helvola', a prolific little plant with finely marked leaves. There are also a number of water-lilies whose flowers tend to change in colour as they age. The flowers of 'Indiana', for example, open a shade of orange-red and then deepen to a coppery red. 'Paul Hariot' has blooms which begin a pale yellow and change to shades of red, while 'Sioux' has yellow flowers which darken to peach. All the plants are on the small side and will do best with about 45 cm. of water over their crowns.

These plants are representative of any selection of water-lilies held by commercial growers. There are many more plants from which to choose and there is no substitute for actually seeing any particular species in bloom. But I would stress the importance of matching your choice of plant with the depth of your pond. This way you will get the best results from your water-lily. Resist the temptation to fall in love with a plant whose needs are not met by your particular pond.

In America, cross-breeding of tropical water-lilies has produced many spectacular results. Unlike the hardy varieties, tropical lilies and their hybrids are often extremely fertile and this has given rise to many hundreds of cultivars. Sadly, their brilliant colours and often superb fragrance are the prerogatives of warm climates. In some Mediterranean areas it is possible to grow tropical water-lilies outdoors in summer and to keep the tubers in damp sand (young tubers or eyes have the best chance of surviving) during the winter. Alternatively, the plant can be treated as an annual, new stock being bought each spring, or you may succeed in raising the plant from seed. Few tropical lilies will grow well in water which is below 21°C. So it is difficult to obtain consistent results in Britian and indeed in much of Europe. A conservatory pool, perhaps with the addition of artificial heat, may be the only answer. But if you live in an area with a consistently high summer temperature, then tender lilies can be started into growth in a glass house in early spring and placed in the outdoor pool later. When the leaves die back towards the end of summer,

that is the time to lift the plant and attempt to winter it in damp sand, well away from rodents, incidentally, which are partial to lily tubers. Free circulation of air is important too during storage, so cover whatever container you use with wire mesh but do not seal it. A comparatively cool temperature is best during storage: 10—15°C. Tropical lilies are rich feeders and need plenty of space but little water over the crown. A half-and-half mixture of well rotted cow manure and loam is ideal. Temperature apart, tender water-lilies are no more difficult to grow than hardy ones. Among day-blooming tropical lilies, the light blue *Nymphaea stellata* (p.62) stands a good chance of blooming in less than the best conditions. And *Nymphaea caerula*, another light blue, may remain open after dark if the temperature remains sufficiently high.

57

58

LEFT *An indoor tropical pool showing the heating system. The large, deep pit in the middle is used for planting the Victoria lily (Victoria amazonica), a hungry feeder. Tropical Nymphaea are grown in baskets around the pool. Note how shallow the pool is (about 45 cm. deep) compared with ponds designed to grow temperate lilies.* BELOW LEFT *The massive Victoria amazonica in flower in the same pool. (National Botanic Gardens, Dublin)*

BELOW *Flower and leaves of the little Water Fringe, Villarsia nymphoides. The flower is only slightly larger than the area enclosed by a thumb and forefinger.*

BOTTOM *The flower and leaf of the Water Hawthorn Aponogeton distachyus. You will extend the flowering season within your pond by including this fine plant.*

It in fact opens in the early morning and will remain open for fifteen hours or more in a favourable climate.

What goes for the tender water-lilies goes also for the *Nelumbo (Nelumbium)* or Lotus, except the lotus requires a longer growing season in order to survive and will not set seed easily. Plants will not necessarily succumb to cold. In fact *Nelumbo* is fairly hardy, although it should be protected from frost. It is because in northerly climates the growing season is short that *Nelumbo* may fail, the tubers becoming weak through undernourishment. The tubers should be planted horizontally, or the lotus can be propagated from nodes taken from the extensive runners which may reach 7 or 10 metres in length in a single season. This is a good reason for growing Nelumbos in round containers, as there is less chance of the runners bunching up as they always do at the corner of square containers. Nodes taken from runners must be kept moist and warm. In America, a native form thrives particularly in the central states and around the Great Lakes. In Southern Europe the lotus does well, and open-air cultivation is certainly possible within the vine-growing districts — and as far north as Vienna. But so far as Britain is concerned, it is really a conservatory or hot house plant, not one for the outdoor pond. Their broad, stately leaves and height — they can be as tall as a man — means they are superbly ornamental, particularly perhaps when grown in large tubs around a patio. This might be one way of growing them in the open in Britain for a month or two, if you can conceive of a means of transporting a heavy tub from a hot house to the patio and back.

The lotus has a magnificent flower not unlike a paeony. The American lotus, *Nelumbo lutea*, has pale, sulphur yellow flowers which can be as much as 25 cm. across. *Nelumbo flavescens* is very similar to *lutea;* it is a more prolific bloomer but the flowers are not quite so large. Still sometimes called the Egyptian Lotus (which would appear to have been a *Nymphaea* in fact), the Indian Lotus, *Nelumbo nucifera* (p.62), is a more vigorous plant than *lutea* and produces even larger flowers of vivid rose which becomes paler with age. The leaves are glabrous, that is, they possess a whitish bloom which gives the green of the leaves a silvery sheen. There are many cultivars including double and dwarf forms: *N. alba* 'Plena' and *N. pygmaea* 'Alba' in white and available in rich pink too. Among the best *Nelumbos* are *N. japonica* 'Rubra' with massive double flowers, 30 cm. across and fragrant; *N.* 'Kermesiana', another Japanese form with flowers of the lightest pink, and *N.* 'Osiris' which bears cup-shaped flowers of very rich pink.

Before turning our attention to marginal plants, two very hardy and easily grown deep-water aquatics deserve to be considered. Water Fringe (called variously *Villarsia nymphoides, Nymphoides peltata, Limnathemum peltatum* and *L. nymphoides*) has heart-shaped leaves rather like a water-lily, but much smaller. They are about 5 cm. across, crinkled at the edges and attractively mottled with purple. A plain-leafed version is available in 'Bennettii'. In late summer, the Water Fringe bears little yellow trumpet flowers held a few centimetres above the surface. The individual blooms do not last long, but a plant can bear a fair number over a long period. Water Fringe, despite its name, is as happy in 60 or 90 cm. of water as it is in a shallow pool. In fact, under any conditions it is a rampant plant and so is best kept in a container. The other deep-water aquatic is extremely popular and deservedly so. It is the Water Hawthorn or *Aponogeton distachyus*. It has long strap-like leaves of dark green or brown and it bears soft white flowers with jet black anthers. In frost-free ponds, flowering will continue well into the winter months. From deep-water aquatics, we now turn to marginal plants.

Nymphaea 'Marliacea Chromatella'

△ *Nymphaea stellata cyanea*

▽ *Nelumbo nucifera*

△ *Nymphaea* 'Froebeli'   ▽ *Nymphaea* 'James Brydon'

5 MARGINAL PLANTS FOR THE POOL

If you are fortunate enough to live in the country or enjoy tramping across the countryside around lakes and natural ponds and rivers, you can hardly have failed to notice how plants grow in their natural habitats. Frequently a number of species will grow in profusion together, inter-mixed in a haphazard fashion. But you will also see, especially if you follow a river for any distance, that at one spot a particular plant flourishes only to disappear completely round the next bend where another kind has taken hold. This in its turn vanishes and on the far bank a third plant has colonized, and so on. And so it should be in a pond. In a confined space, plants which are mixed together only create a confused vision. Similarly, one specimen of ten plants, planted one after the other, will present a scheme lacking in character. What one should aim for is a mass of one plant followed by a showy mass of another. Almost all marginal plants are easily propagated by division, so even if you obtain only one specimen initially, within a season or two you can easily achieve the right effect. Firm, definite groupings of a few plants is very much more desirable than a hotch-potch of many.

Marginal plants, for want of a definition, are those which grow in shallow water or in

Nymphaea, Elodea, Caltha palustris and Iris pseudacorus in a peaceful and uncluttered scheme.

soil that is saturated in water. They have a flowering period which ranges from early spring until autumn. One plant precedes all. That is the lovely *Caltha palustris,* often called Marsh Marigold or Kingcup. I do not think there is any other waterside plant that has given me more pleasure. There comes one of those early spring days when the breeze carries the heady smell of new growth. A new warmth pervades the air and there on the edge of the pool the Marsh Marigold has opened her brilliant yellow flowers. The quality of that yellow seems to me unequalled. I can picture now, in my mind's eye, spring evenings when the sun has just passed over the pond and the flower of the Marsh Marigold seems almost luminous against the dank brown that still remains of last year's growth. The Marsh Marigold produces a mass of flowers that will remain in flower for several weeks. (I also grow the lilac-flowering *Rhododendron* 'Praecox' and masses of the early *Erica* 'Springwood White', so that new life around the pool begins not long after the New Year.) The Marsh Marigold abounds throughout Europe and parts of North America. It reaches a height of about 30 cm., grows best in moist soil or very shallow water and is easily propagated by seed or division. A double variety, *Caltha palustris flore pleno,* is slightly smaller and less vigorous, but it can produce such a wealth of flowers as to almost conceal the plant beneath

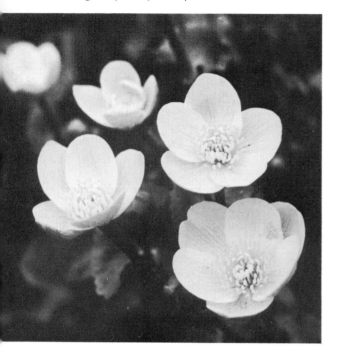

them. An altogether larger version is available in *Caltha polypetala* which grows up to 60 or 90 cm. And from the Himalayas comes a small white version, *Caltha palustris alba,* which may grow no more than 15 or 20 cm. high. These are all excellent plants for concealing an unsightly piece of concrete margin. In shallow water, their generally bushy habit will obscure the margin behind, while planted around the pool, some of the leaves will tend, conveniently, to flop informally over the edge of the bank.

Equally suitable for hiding a few metres of ugly margin is the Bog Bean, or *Menyanthes trifoliata* (p.103), so called because its light green leaves are divided into three well-defined parts. Growing about 30 cm. high, the Bog Bean has a horizontal rootstock and enjoys stretching across the surface of the water

LEFT AND BELOW *Single and double flowers of the Marsh Marigold, Caltha palustris.*

rather like a floating plant. And even if you have no margin that needs concealing, the Bog Bean is well worth growing for its unique flowers. They come just about the time the Marsh Marigold is on the wane or is over. Conspicuous rich pink buds peel back to reveal five snowy white petals which are crested on their surface with long, curly white hairs and these give the flower a fluffy or even a frosty appearance. This is certainly a flower worth examining closely. Look at how snugly the stamens fit around the base of the petals, each with their bright yellow pollen load, and how the light green style protrudes just above the level of the curling hairs. There is no daintier flower among the marginals; a watchmaker might baulk at constructing anything so delicate. Common to many boglands throughout Europe, Asia and North America, *Menyanthes trifoliata* is a plant of vigorous growth but one that can be cut back easily.

Brass Buttons, or *Cotula coronopifolia,* is another plant that enjoys scrambling about the margin in shallow water. The flower consists of a small disc of matt yellow, in itself not very exciting, but where there are tens of these flowers appearing together, as they do during the summer, the effect is lovely. The flowers bend over slightly on top of their thin, elegant stems, looking like so many miniature periscopes. The plant is unlikely to exceed 25 cm. in height. In winter it may die back altogether, as an annual, in which case you are dependent upon the seeds. So do not renew the soil in the basket or around the margin until the new plants have come up the following spring. In the Southern Hemisphere, in South Africa and Australia, where *Cotula coronopifolia* is a native, it can tend to be rather invasive. In more temperate zones it can be introduced safely.

The same cannot be said about the Great Water Plantain, *Alisma plantago-aquatica,* a plant common throughout parts of the Northern Hemisphere. Grown in moist soil or shallow water, it is far from fussy; it throws up elliptic, erect leaves on long stalks, reaching a height of anything from 30 to 90 cm. In mid to late summer appear the tiny nondescript pink or white flowers. What makes the plant so attractive is the pyramidal panicle upon which the flowers appear. Less attractive is the Water Plantain's habit of setting seed anywhere and everywhere. If you introduced this plant then be sure to cut out the panicles as soon as the flowers are over. A more suitable form, because less rampant, is *Alisma lanceolatum* which has long slender leaves and height of about 30-40 cm. But it is also rarer and you may not find it easy to obtain.

No such problem should arise with the popular little Bog Arum, *Calla palustris,* and since it grows no more than 25 cm. in height and is compact in habit it is an obvious choice for the small pool. It thrives with 5 cm. of water over its crown and produces a small white trumpet flower in summer. Comes the autumn and the flowers have been replaced by fruits of brilliant scarlet. A more familiar arum is *Zantedeschia aethiopica* (also known as *Calla aethiopica* and *Richardia africana*) or Arum Lily which grows to a height of 60 to 90 cm. and bears magnificent trumpet flowers of pure white with a yellow 'poker' or spadix within. This plant is not really hardy however, and should be wintered in a cold house which is frost-free. Alternatively, if you experience only mild frosts, the Arum Lily should survive in the pool the whole year round if it has 20 or 30 cm. of water above its crown. Another plant with white trumpet-shaped flowers is to be had in *Lysichitum camtschatcense.* Whether it be planted in moist soil or shallow water this plant does require deep soil: 50 cm. is not

Arum lilies along a river bank

LEFT *The Bog Arum – Calla palustris.* BELOW *Veronica beccabunga or Brooklime.* ABOVE *Lysichiton americanum, which produces light yellow flowers. The leaves, when young, are of a vivid light green.*

too much. Once established it is a difficult plant to lift intact. Raising the plant from seed is rather easier though several years must elapse before the young plants can be expected to flower. The leaves, which vary from 30 to 100 cm. in length, arise almost stemless from the base of the plant. Even when the plant does not attain its maximum height, I find its broad leaves rather too bulky in appearance for a small, compact pool. It looks best when one has plenty of space and other shrubby plants with which it can harmonize. This applies even more to the somewhat taller and broader *Lysichitum americanum* or False American Skunk Cabbage. However, where space permits, this plant produces a welcome contrast to *camtschatcense* and indeed *Calla palustris* in bearing yellow trumpets.

White and yellow are common colours among marginal flowers, whereas blue is comparatively rare. The prostate and rambling *Veronica beccabunga* or Brooklime produces small blue flowers on racemes in the leaf axils. Grow the plant if you would like to try the leaves as a

Water Mint has a whorl of soft lilac-blue flowers.

spring salad, but it has to be said that so far as the flowers are concerned they are rather dull and inconspicuous. A much more brilliant blue is to be had in the Water-Forget-Me-Not or *Myosotis scorpioides (palustris)* and especially in the improved 'Mermaid' strain. The plant varies very much in height, but 20 cm. would be about average; it flowers profusely over a long period and sets seed easily, so that you should have a fine mass of this showy little marginal in a matter of a few seasons. And it thrives in shade. Quite a few plants have been called Forget-Me-Nots from time to time, but the water plant has the greatest claim to the name on account of being named such by German botanists way back in the Middle Ages. But there are more romantic accounts of how the *Myosotis* received its name. One such legend, from the sixteenth century, tells the story of a knight who was taking a stroll with his lady-love along the banks of the River Danube on the eve of their wedding. The lady, to her distress, spotted a spray of these flowers being carried away by the river. Instantly the knight plunged into the river to retrieve them. He reached the flowers only to find that the current was too strong for him to return to the shore. As he was swept by his lady-love he threw the fatal flowers on to the bank beside her, with the exclamation: *'Vergiss mich nicht!'* — 'Forget-me-not!' It is said too that youths in medieval times garlanded their loved ones with chains of Forget-Me-Nots.

The plant is small enough for the smallest pond and conspicuous enough for the largest. For the same reason Water Mint or *Mentha aquatica* should have a place in any water scheme. It will grow in damp soil or under several centimetres of water. The leaves are rather hairy and are found in two colours, a dark maroon colour and a bright green. In the wild, it is commonly found in wetlands adjacent to rivers and lakes, and you will often find plants with both these colours living within a few metres of each other, and sometimes both colours on the one plant. A keen observer will easily discover why. In shade, where the plant does well, the leaves remain green, but when exposed to sunlight for any length of time they soon turn to a purplish maroon hue. Under very favourable conditions Water Mint can reach a height in excess of a metre. But in a confined space the likely

BELOW AND RIGHT *Flower and leaf of the Pickerel Weed,*
Pontederia cordata.

height is about 30 cm. Keep a sufficient number of the plants from which to pluck off leaves to flavour your potatoes. And enjoy the bright whorls of lilac-blue flowers that appear at the end of the summer.

Blue flowers are also produced by the Pickerel Weed or *Pontederia cordata,* some say the best blue flowers of all water plants. But the flowers apart, this is a handsome plant by any standards, sending up light green cordate or heart-shaped leaves on long stalks, and rising 45-75 cm. above water level. It does best in water no more than 12 cm. above its crown, and towards the end of summer the flowers appear on spikes. Not all the flowers on any one spike will necessarily open at the one time, which can give the spike a slightly moth-eaten appearance, it seems to me. But when the Pickerel Weed is grown in sufficient numbers, the individual spikes give way to a mass effect of medium blue. *Pontederia lanceolata* has, as the name suggests, rather more lance-shaped leaves and it grows very much larger, often to 1.5 metres in height, but this species is not fully hardy.

Even more dramatic than the lance-shaped leaves of the *Pontederia* are the arrowhead-shaped leaves of *Sagittaria sagittifolia.* The plant, also known as Common Arrowhead, is best stood in 10-15 cm. of water but it will often thrive in greater depths. The roots need confining as they are stoloniferous and spread

LEFT *Sagittaria sagittifolia, Common Arrowhead.* BELOW LEFT *Japanese Arrowhead, Sagittaria japonica flore pleno.*

rapidly. Occasionally some of the leaves may float on the water, but generally they rise, more or less perpendicularly, 40 cm. above the water surface. The white flowers are produced in midsummer. A larger variety comes in *Sagittaria japonica*, but the one to obtain, if at all possible, is the double form, *Sagittaria japonica flore pleno*, which grows to much the same size as the Common Arrowhead but much more slowly, and there is no need to contain the roots. And the flowers are so double as to seem almost like small snowballs. For effective foliage and flowers this plant should rank high on any choice list of water plants.

Effective foliage is a good reason for growing *Ranunculus lingua* (especially the larger *grandiflora* form), which often reaches a metre in height. Green sword-shaped leaves come off a broad stem knuckled like bamboo and flushed with a hue of dark pink. Ranunculus comes from the Latin name for frog, *Rana*, an allusion to the fact that many of the species inhabit wet places. As the common name of the plant, Tongue Buttercup, implies, it produces flowers very like the common buttercup of the meadow that we all picked as children, only in the *grandiflora* form, they are somewhat larger — often exceeding 5 cm. across. The plant can be expected to flower throughout the summer and even into the autumn. On account of its rather thin flower stems, however, the plant can look rather gangly and

Ranunculus lingua – Tongue Buttercup

windswept after stormy weather. If you have a sheltered corner, place it there in shallow water, and contain the stoloniferous roots which can send up shoots at a considerable distance from the parent plant.

Less susceptible to wind is *Butomus umbellatus* or Flowering Rush. It grows to much the same height as the Tongue Buttercup, around a metre, and thrives in water up to 10 cm. deep. The long, thin leaves are shaped rather like stilettoes and are occasionally twisted. In midsummer come the flowers, sometimes light pink, sometimes almost maroon. Rising from their stalks, the whole flower head resembles the structure of an inverted umbrella,

ABOVE *Planting a fine specimen of the Tongue Buttercup, Ranunculus lingua grandiflora.*

LEFT *The flower head of the Water Gladiole, Butomus umbellatus.*

73

LEFT *The Branched Bur Reed, Sparganium erectum. This photograph well illustrates its fine structure. The large burs are the female flowers, the smaller ones above are the male ones.*
BELOW *Close-up of the flowers of the Golden Club, Orontium aquaticum.*

hence the name *umbellatus*. A single umbel may produce as many as thirty flowers. The plant is found in Europe and Asia, and its colourfulness and shape make it an obvious choice for the garden pond.

Some gardeners feel the Bur Reed or *Sparganium erectum* is not a plant worth including in the garden. True, its strap-like leaves which rise from the base in two distinct ranks are not of great interest and the flowers are not

Typha latifolia

colourful. Nevertheless, the flowers, the large female burs and the smaller male ones, do create an unusual design unlike any other plant. So if you have a keen eye for structure this is a plant you might care to grow. It is quite happy to stand in water of any depth up to 45 cm., a useful feature since few other plants will tolerate that depth. However, if you have but one bay of that depth, then the Bur Reed should hardly be your first choice.

That distinction should surely go to the Golden Club, *Orontium aquaticum*, a versatile and highly spectacular plant. The leaves are of a dark velvety green on their upper side and of a silvery sheen underneath. When planted in deep water the leaves tend to float, whereas in moist soil at the pond's edge — where the plant will do equally well — the leaves grow more or less upright to a height of about 45 cm. Then, of course, the contrasting shades of the leaves can be appreciated to the full, especially when a light breeze creates a shimmering effect. In spring and early summer, the Golden Club produces a large number of strikingly white stems or spadices, at the ends of which appear the bright yellow flowers. The effect is of a brilliant white matchstick with a yellow head. Matchsticks however, do not come 30 cm. long and as thick as your finger. So it is both the size and colour of the flowers as well as the leaves which make the Golden Club so fine a waterside plant. It does

have the disadvantage of requiring deep soil, 45 cm. at least, and once established the plant can only be lifted with difficulty. Propagate by seed, starting them in shallow water.

Everyone who owns a pond will want to grow *Typha,* and with good reason. The long rush-like leaves and the tall brown pokers of the Reed Mace or Bulrush as *Typha* is commonly called, are for most people inseparable from water. The question is which *Typha* to grow. The commonly found *Typha latifolia* is a magnificent plant, but one which can produce a veritable forest of vegetation two or more metres in height. Clearly this is only a plant for lakes and very large water schemes. The more slender *Typha angustifolia* can reach a similar height, but will remain somewhat shorter if kept within bounds and it should still flower reasonably well. In the wild, the two plants can be distinguished by the fact that the leaves of *Typha latifolia* are mostly 1 cm. or more in width, while those of *Typha angustifolia* do not usually exceed 0.5 cm. Shorter species of Reed Mace, namely *Typha Shuttleworthii* and *Laxmanii* are perhaps more suited to the garden pool, but these plants are not so easy to come by. So, for most gardeners, the best choice is *Typha minima*, a dwarf species unlikely to exceed 50 cm. in height. This little plant does have a drawback, however. Its flowers are not so elongated and so are less poker-like than are those of the other species. Sometimes, in fact, the flowers of *T. minima* are almost globular. The mace is the symbol of kingship; and the name Reed Mace derives from the fact that Rubens and early Italian painters depicted, in their *Ecce Homo* paintings, the crucified Christ holding the *Typha* reed in one hand. The reed has also a place in Greek mythology. In one legend, the God Apollo, so incensed at King Midas preferring the singing of another to his own, clapped a pair of ass's ears upon the unfortunate king. The king's barber discovered them and felt quite unable to contain so awful a secret. So he hid the secret at the foot of a clump of bulrushes. The reeds could not contain the secret either, and while rustling gently in the breeze, kept murmuring: 'King Midas has ass's ears'. Provided your children are at an age when they can treat fire sensibly, the pokers of the Bulrush can make dramatic torches at a barbecue. Cut the pokers down at the base and allow them to dry indoors. Then soak their heads in paraffin or methylated spirits. Placed in holders around the pond they make a spectacular, if shortlived, form of illumination.

The name bulrush, a corruption of Pool Rush, really refers to *Scirpus lacustris,* a broad and tall plant, too invasive for consideration in a garden. And much as one might admire the dark green, triangular foliage of *Scirpus maritimus* of universal distribution, it is much too vigorous for any setting other than the largest. To be sure, it is a fine plant for

A well-designed patio pond, with herbaceous borders.

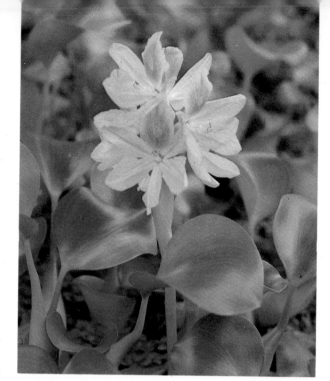

Eichhornia crassipes ▷

▽ *Trapa natans*

For growing conditions of the Water Hyacinth, Eichhornia crassipes, and the Water Chestnut, Trapa natans, see pages 43–4.

The Porcupine Quill Rush, Scirpus tabernaemontani zebrinus, showing some stems reverting to their plain state.

attracting wild fowl to your pond. It provides them with excellent cover. But let it be emphasized, water-lilies and choice aquatics are not compatible with ducks, which will eat all before them. For the ornamental pond, the obvious choice from the *Scirpus* genus is *Scirpus Tabernaemontani zebrinus*. The plant is known variously as the Porcupine Quill Rush on account of its smooth, slender and sharply pointed leaves, and as the Zebra Rush on account of its very distinctive cream and white bands which ring each leaf from top to bottom. This feature is unique in the plant kingdom. Plant in clumps in shallow water and this rush will grow to about 1.4 metres and will be a most conspicuous element in any pond, especially when the surface of the water is quite still and the bands are doubled by reflection. Should any plain green leaves appear, these should be cut out in case the plant intends to revert to its unvariegated state. Propagation is easily achieved by division. For a striped, rather than a banded effect, include a clump of Manna Grass or *Glyceria aquatica variegata (Glyceria spectabilis)*. It possesses narrow, grass-like foliage striped with no less than three colours: green, yellow and white; in fact four colours, because in spring and autumn a rosy tint creeps into the foliage. In a small basket this lovely plant may grow no more than 30 cm. high. When given all the space it requires, Manna Grass will reach a height of about 90 cm. It spreads rapidly in shallow water and moist soil, so it is as well to restrict its roots.

There are one or two species from the *Juncus* genus which are worth including in the pond. The majority are, as a rule, far too vigorous and tenacious to introduce with safety. The first exception is *Juncus effusus spiralis* which, unlike its relations, is a comparatively modest grower. It is a curiosity plant and the delight of any child. Its leaves grow in wiry spirals, often with the uniformity of a corkscrew. Old timers nicknamed it 'Harry Lauder's walking-

LEFT *A leaf cut off the Corkscrew Rush, Juncus effusus spiralis. The leaves grow in a tangled mass, but many of them have the symmetry of a corkscrew.*

BELOW *Florets of Juncus ensifolius.*

stick', for it does rather resemble the crooked walking-stick of that famous Scottish comedian. The second exception is *Juncus ensifolius* which grows 30-50 cm. high. The foliage is rather undistinguished, but towards the end of the summer the plant produces little brown florets which at a distance appear as jet black. They might be the brooms of some miniature chimney sweep. Shallow water or moist soil suits both plants.

If you have a flower arranger in the house, a planting of Sweet Galingale, *Cyperus longus,* will be appreciated, for it is a favourite source of greenery for the florist's art. Its dark green, slender stems which rise perfectly straight for most of their length and then gracefully curve over, make excellent background material. And you need never fear cutting off too many of the stems. Sweet Galingale is a trenchant plant and will throw up large numbers of these decorative stems year in year out. The bulbous root, incidentally, is edible. Another highly decorative plant in this genus is *Cyperus alternifolius* or Umbrella Grass. As a native of Madagascar it is not fully hardy, so it should be grown in a basket and wintered indoors. Apart from that, the plant is not fussy, being equally content either in shallow water or on the bank. It grows to about 90 cm.

If you have a summer-house with a wooden or stone floor, then by growing the Sweet Flag, *Acorus calamus,* you can revive an ancient

RIGHT *The Sweet Flag, Acorus calamus variegatus, showing its peculiar flower spike. The variegated form, incidentally, has slightly less aroma than the unvariegated one.*

BELOW *The Umbrella Grass – Cyperus alternifolius*

custom. Crush the leaves and they will impart a pleasant perfume not unlike a tangerine orange. This feature of the plant made it highly sought after for strewing over the floor in medieval and Renaissance times. As the leaves were crushed by being walked upon, so the great halls and rooms of olden times were filled with the Flag's sweet aroma. At least so we may believe was the case on occasion, but not always. When the great scholar Erasmus visited Oxford around the end of the fifteenth century, he was not enamoured to find that the rushes on the floors harboured 'expectorations, vomitings, the leakage of dogs and men, ale-droppings, scraps of fish'. But so fond was Cardinal Wolsey of the Sweet Flag that he had the strewings at his palace, Hampton Court, renewed daily. Such extravagance brought the cardinal much criticism. Moist soil or shallow water suit the Sweet Flag equally well and in either situation it grows to about 70 cm. A Japanese variety, *Acorus gramineus,* grows to about half the height of *calamus.* Variegated forms of both are available, the young leaves being vividly striped in green and creamy yellow, fading somewhat to a paler colour in late summer.

When Sweet Flag was in short supply or unobtainable, the odourless Yellow Flag was used instead. Although only second best as a floor strewing, the Yellow Flag has had a rather more elevated history than the Sweet Flag, since Louis VII of France took its lovely flower for use as an armorial device. For this reason it is known as 'Fleur de Louis' as well as 'Fleur de Luce' and 'Fleur de Lis'. Around Orleans in France arose a curious legend whereby it was believed that the seventh son in a family with no daughters intervening, known as a marcon, had somewhere on his body the imprint of the Fleur de Louis and possessed magical powers. Whoever was suffering from 'king's evil' or scrofula had only

ABOVE *Iris sibirica* RIGHT *Iris pseudoacorus* – Yellow Flag

to touch this imprint or even be breathed upon by the marcon and his malady would disappear.

The Latin name for Yellow Flag is *Iris pseudacorus,* a name presumably chosen to signify its similarity to *Acorus calamus.* The two plants are often found together in the same boggy situations and along river banks, but they are not so similar in appearance. *Acorus* has dark green leaves, comparatively thin and strap-like, often with undulations appearing along the edges for a short distance. The leaves of *Iris pseudacorus* are light green with a distinctive blueish tinge and they are shaped like many sword blades standing with their tips upwards. Although the flowers of this iris, like that of almost all irises, evoke a supreme sense of fineness and delicacy, the plant itself is very robust. Possessing a tough and vigorous rhizome, *Iris pseudacorus* is to be found in large numbers in many rivers and wetlands throughout Europe and beyond. If you include it in your pond an energetic programme of cutting back will be necessary from time to time. A more modest grower is found in *Iris pseudacorus variegatus* with its cream and green stripes running the length of the leaf. It has the same flower as the unvariegated form, while a lighter, lemon yellow flower is produced by *Iris pseudacorous bastardi.* Seeds from the ordinary plant very occasionally produce *bastardi.* The plant has the advantage of being unusual if not rare, but the flowers are much less conspicuous than those of the common form. From North America comes *Iris versicolor,* or Blue Flag, which is almost identical to *Iris pseudacorous* except the flowers are purplish-blue instead of yellow. All these irises will do well in wet soil or shallow water and they grow up to a metre in height.

The smaller blue *Iris sibircia* with its grass-like foliage is a particularly versatile plant. It will grow in an herbaceous border with a reasonably high moisture content as well as

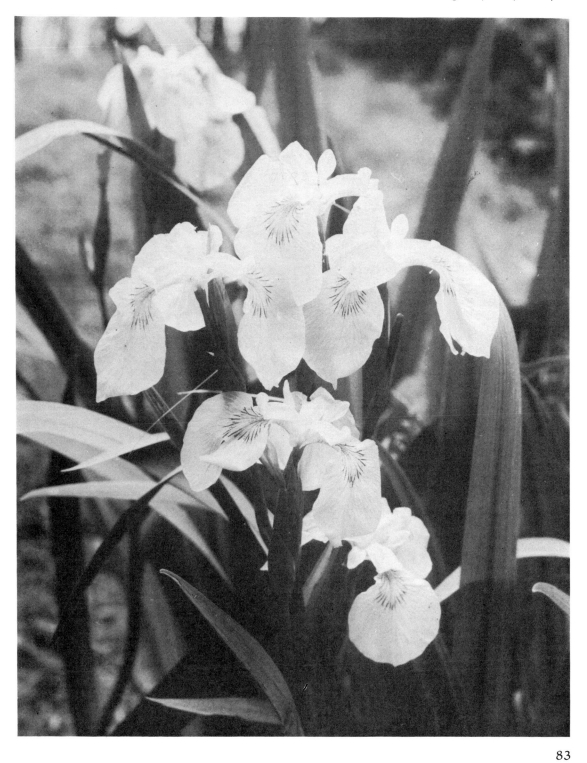

in a basket submerged in the pond provided its crown is no more than barely covered with water. There are several cultivars of this iris ranging from the deep purple of 'Caesar' to the pure white of 'Snow Queen'. For deeper water, up to 10 cm. above the crown, grow the true water-loving *Iris laevigata*, or *Iris kaempferi*. These two plants need to be distinguished, because whereas *laevigata* relishes water over its crown throughout the year, *kaempferi* does not. *Kaempferi* comes from the rice fields of Japan which are flooded during the summer months and are no more than

moist during the winter ones. By growing *kaempferi* in a basket, it can be placed in the pool in spring once growth has begun and removed in autumn. Otherwise try to find a spot which is boggy but not totally saturated. There are a number of ways in which *Iris kaempferi* and *laevigata* can be differentiated. The leaves of *kaempferi* have a distinctive raised mid-rib which can be easily felt and which *laevigata* lacks (the name *laevigata* comes from the Latin for smooth). The standards of *kaempferi* never exceed two thirds the length of the falls and are often shorter than that.

Iris laevigata

The falls are very broad — the plant's most conspicuous feature — and they often stretch out almost horizontally. The seeds of *kaempferi* are flat, circular or nearly circular discs, contained in a capsule no more than 2.5 cm. long. In *Iris laevigata* the standards and falls are roughly of equal length. The seeds are semi-circular and contained in capsules 5 cm. long. Both these plants require a rich, loamy soil. *Kaempferi* does not like soil that contains chalk or lime while in winter it will appreciate an occasional dose of liquid manure. Propagation is easily achieved by seed or division. Seeds planted in autumn should germinate the following spring, but it may be several years before flowers are produced. It is a good idea to remove the seed capsules in autumn whether or not you intend using the seeds, as this will encourage flowering in the following year.

All these marginal plants can be grown in the pond. Many of them can, as pointed out, be grown in moist soil around it. But there are many more moisture-loving plants which will not tolerate saturated soil. To grow these plants one must think in terms of a bog garden.

The flowers of single and double kaempferi irises, showing the characteristic broad falls and short standards.

6 VIRTUES AND VICES OF A BOG GARDEN

A bog garden is most often envisaged as simply and extension of the pond. That, after all, is the way it is with nature. Around most lakes and natural ponds lies a boggy area where moisture-loving plants abound. But a gardener, especially the species known as the weekend gardener, should perhaps take a different view. If high on your list of priorities is that your water garden should involve little maintenance and care, then you would be well advised to install a pond only. A bog garden is of course labour intensive. Moist soil is a haven for weeds. There are a number of bog plants that can hold their own against grass and weeds blown in on the wind, *Eriophorum* and *Hemerocallis*, for example; but even a 'wild' bog garden will need more tending than the pool. And besides, a bog garden of this sort will only look right in a large informal setting where there are trees and shrubs to act as a natural backdrop.

There are other considerations too. Bog plants will, obviously, only survive as long as the soil is kept sufficiently moist. If you live in an area of hot, dry summers, maintaining moisture in the soil may be a constant problem, especially if water rationing is involved. A pond and its inhabitants, animal and vegetable, can endure even if the water level drops drastically. Marginals planted in baskets will

Bog Cotton, Eriophorum angustifolium, is a conspicuous plant which is easily grown in wet or damp acid soil.

survive as long as the bottom of the baskets remain in water. (A pond which actually dries up is too shallow in the first place.) But the same weather conditions which would simply lower a well-designed pond, might will dry up the bog garden. And where space is limited I would not be inclined to forego a conventional rockery in favour of a bog garden. A rockery which contains heathers and dwarf conifers — whatever else it may contain — can provide colour and leaf in winter when the bog garden and pond have little to offer.

That is the negative way of looking at a bog garden. In its favour it can be said that a pond and bog garden combined offer a far more varied scheme of gardening, the range of plants is greatly extended; and for anyone who is prepared to involve himself in the additional maintenance, the results can be very brilliant indeed. There is also the advantage that a good number of bog plants are tolerant of shade. This is worth bearing in mind if you have a shady corner close to the pond. If you live in an area of high summer rainfall, the soil round the pond may remain quite moist or damp through most of the year, and the occasional flooding of the pond should therefore satisfy the moisture requirements of most bog plants. Otherwise there are two ways of making a bog garden.

One way is to dig out the site for the pond large enough to include a bog area as well.

A bog garden combined with the pond

Across one end of the pond is built a dividing wall. This is best done in a concrete pond, but it is not out of the question to build a wall on liners such as Butyl rubber and PVC. One needs to use mortar rather than concrete, i.e. cement and sand but no coarse, sharp aggregate. (The base will need to be broad because the wall will have little or no purchase at either end.) Placing an extra strip of liner under the wall is a sensible precaution. This dividing wall should not be waterproof, but all it needs are just a few small holes to allow water to seep through from the pond without soil passing the other way. The area for the bog garden should be filled with sand (for liner ponds), cinders, gravel, etc., to about 30 cm. from the top of the wall. Above this should be built a mixture of loam, well-rotted cow manure, leafmould or peat, and sand. The loam should make up about half the mixture, and the others should each make up about one sixth of the total. For bog plants which will not tolerate their roots standing in water, build up the bog garden in a form of a rockery at least 30 cm. above the water table. A great advantage of this particular form of bog garden is that it does not have to be watered separately from the pond. Just top up the pond and automatically the moisture content of the bog garden is maintained. But there are disadvantages. Firstly, the rate of evaporation from the pond will be greatly accelerated. The surface of the soil will pass water to the surrounding air and draw up more moisture from the pond at a surprising rate. And that is not to mention the needs of the bog plants themselves. For this reason, this kind of bog garden is only possible if you have a comparatively deep pond, say approaching a metre in depth, although a greater depth would be no disadvantage. Secondly, it is important that the actual surface area of the bog garden should be small in proportion to the surface area of the pond, otherwise you will almost be able to watch the water level drop before your eyes in hot weather. Make the bog garden ten or fifteen per cent of the total pool area, no more. This kind of bog garden is obviously best suited to large pools both as regards depth and surface area.

If your pool is a small one, then you would be better advised to use a different type of bog garden, and in a way it is a simpler one. Dig out a trough about 30 cm. deep and line it with polythene or cement, and in either case the lining should *not* be waterproof. Better still, make the trough 45 cm. deep, the lower 15 cm. or so consisting of a 'V' shaped channel running the length of the trough. Holes in the concrete or perforations in the polythene should be made above the level of the 'V'. The idea is that the liner will hold water up to the level of the 'V', but above that it can seep

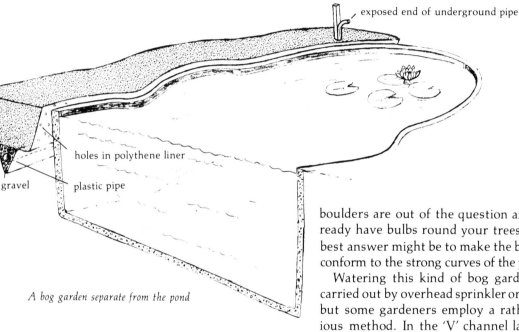

exposed end of underground pipe

holes in polythene liner

gravel   plastic pipe

A bog garden separate from the pond

away to prevent the plants becoming saturated and the soil becoming sour.

This method of making a bog garden offers considerable design possibilities. Do not think simply of digging out a hole adjacent to the pond. If you have it in mind to grow a large number of Primulas, for example, then the bog garden might be designed so as to wend its way round a series of boulders or trees. A circular bog garden with a clump of plants of whatever kind in the vicinity of an informal pond is certain to look artificial. Aim to make the bog garden conform to some specific focal point in the garden or some strong line. If

boulders are out of the question and you already have bulbs round your trees, then the best answer might be to make the bog garden conform to the strong curves of the pond itself.

Watering this kind of bog garden can be carried out by overhead sprinkler or hose pipe, but some gardeners employ a rather ingenious method. In the 'V' channel lay down a length of plastic pipe which contains a series of holes at about 60 cm. intervals. One end of the pipe is sealed off and buried. The other end is left open and above ground. All one has to do now is connect a hose pipe to this underground pipe and the entire bog garden can be watered at the same time. Incidentally, the holes in the underground pipe nearest the inlet should not, if possible, be larger than the holes nearest the stopped end. Otherwise the water pressure may not be evenly distributed. And if you bury the pipe in gravel with the holes facing downwards, the chances of the holes becoming clogged will be minimized.

soil at least 30 cm. deep

rubble

Formal bog beds made by dividing a pond.

retaining wall with small holes at intervals

While a bog garden is usually associated with an informal pond, there is no reason why a formal scheme should not have a formal bog garden , or preferably, to give a more balanced result, several bog gardens. Take, for example, a rectangular pond. About half a metre in from each end could be placed retaining walls to provide two narrow moist beds. Irises look particularly well in a formal design. In the case of a patio pool, bog beds can be sunk in the patio, the bed shape designed to complement the pond. They can be fed by pipe from the pond although this raises the problem of leaking joints. It would be better to join the bog beds to the pond by means of a continuous channel. If the beds are on the same level as the pond then the water level will be the same in both, and this limits one to plants which will tolerate their roots being saturated. Where the pond is a sunken one, then the beds can be placed in the higher ground surrounding the pond. They can still be fed from the pond, of course, but their water table will be lower. Alternatively, the beds can be built up with bricks or cement. The area of the beds below the water table must, of course, be quite waterproof. And to prevent moisture

*Flush and raised bog
gardens connected to the pond.*

seeping out through the bricks above that level, it is as well to line the whole bed with a liner material.

In the case of a bog garden built like a rockery, the soil on the lowest levels will contain the most water. Begin with plantings of Marsh Marigold, of Bog Arum and Forget-Me-Nots and marginals we have already considered. In addition, plantings of *Mimulus* or

Monkey Flowers will provide masses of colour at the pool's edge from summer until the first frosts of autumn. And they will flower even when, through lack of room or soil, they do not attain their full height. *Mimulus* is a primary choice for the small pond. The plant sets seed easily, especially if raised in a cold frame, so that quantities of their showy flowers, rather like open-throated snapdragons,

LEFT TO RIGHT *Mimulus luteus with a plain yellow flower; M. guttatus blotched with red, and hose-in-hose variety.*

can be had in a few seasons. And if that is not praise enough, one can add that *Mimulus* comes in a variety of colours and shapes. Most of the species come from North America, including *Mimulus luteus* which has naturalized itself in Europe. The flowers are yellow. *M. guttatus* is similar except it has reddish blotches or spots on the flowers. Crosses between the two are common. They grow to about 45 cm. but are often a great deal shorter than that. The Monkey Musk, *M. moschatus,* grown for generations for its distinctive perfume, is a creeping plant of low habit. The flowers are pale yellow and not very conspicuous. The plant is mainly suited to very small ponds and has, incidentally, lost its scent. The 'hose-in-hose' varieties are well worth growing, but are not quite as spectacular as *M. cardinalis* whose flowers are a vivid combination of scarlet and yellow. If you want a *Mimulus* that will grow with a few centimetres of water over its crown, then choose *M. ringens,* a species which grows anything from 20 to 90 cm. high and produces flowers of violet or blue. To these, in moist soil, one might add White Bachelor's Buttons *Ranunculus aconitifolius flore pleno,* whose dark green, finely divided leaves will combine beautifully with other plants. And there is a yellow

version, *R. acris flore pleno,* 60 cm. high, which produces lovely double buttercup flowers in profusion throughout the summer.

But for many people the desire to grow bog *Primula* will be the main reason for building a bog garden. *Primula* favour moist, rich but not sodden soil and they certainly dislike sourness. In shade or full sunshine, they can provide a pond with a lightness and gaiety that I do not think is rivalled by any other moisture-loving plant; and they have an ex-

Flowers of the White Bachelor's Buttons

ceptionally long flowering period. They are most effective when grown in large clumps, one colour giving way to another. Propagation may be carried out either by seed or division. Immediately the seedlings have ripened, place them in shallow trays containing two parts of loam, two of leafmould and one of sand. Barely cover them with compost and place the trays in a cold-frame, shielded from strong sunlight if necessary. Germination takes place in about four weeks. The seedlings should be pricked out as soon as they are large enough to be separated easily and placed in outdoor boxes, and from there into the bog garden. Many primulas will seed themselves naturally too, and where cross-fertilization takes place you will find new blends of colour and sometimes spotted or blotched forms.

To begin the season early, plant the small Himalayan *Primula denticulata* which will produce globular clusters of lilac, red or white flowers from March onwards. It is satisfied with a modicum of moisture, so it can be placed in the drier parts of the bog garden. For wet soil, the obvious choice is from the candelabra varieties. *P. japonica,* 45 cm. high, produces up to six tiers of the most vivid red to purple flowers in many shades and there is a white form too. *P. beesiana,* a Chinese bog primula, has the distinction of purplish-red flowers with yellow centres. Both these plants seed themselves very readily. So too does the large *P. pulverulenta,* 90 cm. tall with its many tiers of purple flowers. And there are many hybrids available, including the famous 'Bartley strain' of apricot, buff and many hues of pink (p.103). With the larger pond still in mind, one might add the giant Himalayan Cowslip, *P. florindae,* which also reaches about 90 cm. in height; or what is regarded as a more elegant if less showy form, *P. sikkimensis,* 60 cm. high. The miniaturist might choose the red to lilac *P. frondosa* or the carmine *P. rosea.* Neither of these grows much above 15 cm. But whatever

A bog rim around a circular pond. The outer rim is perfectly waterproof, the inner is not.

For the water's edge, probably the finest fern you can grow is the Royal Fern, *Osmunda regalis*. It does have a regal height, however, and can reach a metre and a half in rich, peaty and moist soil. Better suited to the medium sized pool is *Matteuccia struthiopteris*, or Ostrich Feather Fern, which rarely grows more than 90 cm. high. Its fronds grow upwards in a circular form, looking as much like a giant shuttlecock as the plumage of an ostrich. Its roots are stoloniferous, as are those of *Onoclea sensibilis*, a more vigorous plant though smaller, at 60 cm. on average (in America it is found rather too rampant). It is a fern which will do well in *comparatively* dry situations as

ABOVE *The Royal Fern, Osmunda regalis, situated in partial shade at the water's edge.* RIGHT *An overhead view of Matteuccia struthiopteris.*

varieties or cultivars you select from this large field — and is there such a thing as an ugly primula? — grow them in scores, all of them. Occasionally one sees primulas displayed in something approaching neat rows in botanic gardens. That is a useful scheme where identification is the first requirement. But the effect is rather stark. In a bog garden, primulas are shown to best effect when combined with other plants. Where space permits, the primula makes an excellent partner with hardy ferns, whose cool, peaceful ambience will heighten the primula's brilliance.

well as in wet, provided it is not exposed to too much sunlight. For finely cut fronds of vivid green, one can hardly do better than choose the well-named Lady Fern, *Athyrium filix-femina.* It grows about a metre high in moist, shaded or partially shaded positions. Rather smaller is the Hardy Maidenhair Fern, *Adiantum pedatum,* generally thought of as one of the most beautiful of ferns. It grows 60 cm. high, requires shade and shelter, and like most ferns appreciates soil rich in humus. This is a useful plant for floral decoration. Equally elegant is *Adiantum capillus veneris,* known as the True Maidenhair Fern, which will do best in deep shade. *Thelypteris phegopteris (Phegopteris*

*Sensitive Fern
– Onoclea sensibilis*

*Hardy Maidenhair Fern
– Adiantum pedatum*

*Lady Fern – Athyrium
filix-femina Cristatum*

95

Blechnum tabulare

polypodiodes) is well worth growing for its autumnal foliage, which resembles that of the beech tree, hence its common name of Beech Fern. And for foliage which slowly changes character through the year, the young fronds beginning with a pinkish tinge turning to dark green and then to brown, grow *Blechnum tabulare.* It is well suited to moist or wet conditions.

For the rockery, an easy fern to grow is *Dryopteris dilatata* known under the lengthy title of Broad Prickly-toothed Buckler Fern. It is a fern which suits the larger bog garden since it can reach a metre and a half in height. For compactness and a very satisfying shade of rich green, I would include plantings of the Soft Shield Fern, *Polystichum setiferum,* and it only grows about 70 cm. high; moreover there are a number of fine cultivars from which to choose. Of much the same height is the evergreen fern *Blechnum spicant,* whose fronds are divided into narrow pinnae or leaflets which gives the plant a rather wiry appearance. It is a distinctive feature although not one to create the sort of soothing ambience one associates with ferns. To provide a carpet effect, always useful when combining other low-growing bog plants, you might use *Blechnum penna-marina.* The fronds are of a very dark green and only about 15 cm. long. It has an informal habit, some of the fronds growing upright or partially so, others quite prostrate. The plant is evergreen. And so is the strap-

Polystichum setiferum plumosum

like Hart's Tongue, *Phyllitis scolopendrium,* a fern very common in parts of the British Isles and Ireland. There are many variations of the common form, *cristatum* for example in which the ends of each frond are conspicuously divided; and if you have a rustic bridge, a rocky waterfall, little nooks or crannies in the rockery, then this is the fern with which to fill them. Another is *Polypodium diversifolium,* a native of Australia and New Zealand, with long, finger-like fronds. Many ponds are built in the vicinity of dry stone walls. If you want a dainty fern for such a position, then *Asplenium trichomanes,* the Maidenhair Spleenwort, will meet your need.

Ferns loomed large in folk lore. Once it was believed that the little folk went trysting, borne aloft on aerial steeds made of fronds. Another belief was that whoever could capture the seed of a fern, which made its appearance only at midnight on midsummer's day, would receive magical powers. Ferns also played

LEFT *The Hart's Tongue Fern takes many forms. The buckled appearance of the fronds on this plant is its most distinctive feature.* BELOW LEFT *Blechnum penna-marina, a fern of low habit which makes it useful for rockeries and for combining with other small plants.*

Polypodium diversifolium

a part in love potions (they can be poisonous, in fact). The old beliefs are gone, but to walk through a glade of ferns is to know that their mystical atmosphere remains.

Hosta is another plant that combines well with *Primula*. It likes a rich, deep, moist or damp soil but is not particular as to sun or shade. The plant is grown primarily for its broad and compact leaves, the flowers in many cases being uninteresting and sometimes partly hidden between the leaves. An exception is to be had in *H. ventricosa,* whose large purple to blue flowers rise well above the leaves. But its overall height of 90 cm. makes it rather too large and bulky for many gardens. *H. lancifolia,* 60 cm. high, with dark green though not particularly broad leaves, is more suited to the smaller bog garden. Preference might be given, though, to *H. glauca,* which has glaucous leaves of rich blue, or *H. glauca fortunei* (also called simply *H. fortunei)*

whose leaves are less blue but whose pale lilac blooms appear on top of tall stalks. For dramatic effect, you might choose *H. fortunei marginata alba,* whose dark green leaves are edged with white or cream. This is a most conspicuous plant. Do remember, however, that if you are growing the variegated forms of such plants as *Acorus calamus, Iris pseudacorus, Scirpus* and so on, the effect of green and cream and white, endlessly repeated, can be rather overpowering. One can have too much of a good thing.

The new pond owner almost always overlooks grass-like plants in favour of more colourful ones. This is a pity. They provide the water garden with a dignity few other plants can equal. This is especially true on calm, still days when the reflection of muted colours in the pond will evoke a sense of placidity which irises, for example, by their very colourfulness cannot do. Moreover, plants whose beauty lies in their leaf and shape are of two metres and more — are the largest that can be grown in temperate zones. The plant itself can reach a height of 4.5 metres. A native of Brazil, *Gunnera* is named after J. Ernst Gunner, a versatile individual who combined the roles of bishop and botanist. Doubtless it is the very massiveness of the plant which has made it so popular, although it is not fully hardy. To protect from frost it needs to have its leaves doubled over the crown in the autumn and this will provide it not only with protection but with a mulch. No other treatment is necessary. However, to my mind, unless planted in a spacious garden and unless its site is congenial and the plant attains its

LEFT *The mighty Gunnera manicata well situated on a large expanse of water. Its extraordinary flower spike* BELOW *can be a metre or more in length, and 30 cm. in diameter.*

attractive throughout the whole growing season. If you are not including Sweet Galingale *(Cyperus longus)* in your scheme, then *Carex stricta* or *pendula* will create the same elegant effect. So too will the lovely *C. riparia* 'Bowles' Golden' which needs very wet soil or shallow water and grows no more than 40 cm. high. More than most plants, these sedges will give the impression that your pond has existed for years: they mature the scene. And for the larger scheme, Pampas Grass, *Cortaderia argentea,* has a warming as well as a maturing effect. The plumes are white or silvery and sometimes touched with lavender, while the plumes of the less well known *Cortaderia quila* have a definite lavender hue and are, if anything, even more feathery. They are excellent subjects for reflection close to the pond. Coming from South America they appreciate a certain amount of shelter.

Perhaps no other plant is more often grown where it is ill-suited than the mighty *Gunnera manicata*. Its leaves — which can attain a width

LEFT *Hosta lancifolia*

true proportions, *Gunnera manicata* looks like nothing so much as a rhubarb plant that has got beyond itself. Beside a small or even medium-sized pond, *Gunnera* appears not so much a dominant, imposing plant as a clumsy intruder. It is only in the context of a vast expanse of water that the true magnificence of this plant becomes apparent.

And much the same can be said about the rhubarbs, such as *Rheum palmatum,* whose deeply lobed leaves create a fine impression of opulence on a plant that can reach 2.5 metres and more, and which produces panicles of creamy white flowers. *Rheum palmatum atrosanguineum* has leaves even more deeply dissected and magnificent flowers of brilliant crimson. But the owner of the small garden would be best advised to resist such glories and include a dwarf species such as *Rheum inopinatum,* 60 cm.

high. Not that the compromise is a great one; this little plant has conspicuous red veins and stems with greyish-green leaves and scarlet flowers. *Rheum,* conveniently, likes to be left undisturbed for years and does best in rich, moist soil and some shade. More shade and less moisture suits *Rodgersia,* a genus much admired for both its foliage and flowers. *Rodgersia pinnata alba* has dark brownish-green leaves and white flowers, while *R. pinnata elegans* has a more bronze tint in the foliage and red flowers. As neither of these plants is likely to exceed 60 cm., they can be accommodated in most schemes.

And no bog garden of whatever size should be without a few varieties of *Astilbe.* Few moisture-loving plants are more obliging as regards situation and none is more spectacular. Any soil will satisfy these plants and while

Rodgersia aesculifolia

Astilbe simplicifolia

A striking specimen of Rheum palmatum dominates a pond,
with Astilbes in the foreground.

101

they respond to plenty of moisture in summer, very satisfactory results can be obtained in less than optimum conditions. Their flowers are borne in soft, feathery and pointed plumes. The flowers of the large *Aruncus sylvester (Spirea aruncus)* and the smaller fine-leaved *A. kneiffi* are not dissimilar to those of *Astilbe*. And the flowers of *Rodgersia* and of *Spirea*, although lacking the same pointed tops, are often confused with *Astilbe*. All these plants are well worth growing for their soft, fluffy plumes, as is the Double Meadow-sweet, once classified as a *Spirea* but now called *Filipendula ulmaria plena*. But what can equal the radiance of *Astilbe* blooms caught in the bright sunshine of a summer's day or their soft, glowing colours contained in a shady glade? Astilbes bloom from June to August and varieties abound. There is a fine choice of colours in the *Arendsii* cultivars: pink, red (p.103), white and mauve, ranging in height from 60 cm. to 1.8 metres; and there is

Goat's Beard, *Aruncus sylvester*, makes an effective display by the waterside where space permits.

a little Japanese form, *A. simplicifolia*, which is only 22 cm. high. It produces a little frothy spire of pink flowers. Propagate Astilbes by division.

No less easy to grow is *Hemerocallis*, derived from the Greek 'for a day', hence the common name of Day Lily. Despite the short life of the individual bloom, the Day Lily flowers over a long period, and if a number of different hybrids are planted, one can expect blooms to appear all summer long. They need little or no tending, improve with the years, and they are forceful enough to defeat a multitude of weeds. *Hemerocallis* comes in innumerable hybrids mainly of orange and yellow, but also of pure white. Like *Astilbe*, *Hemerocallis* thrives in moist soil, but I feel these plants should not be placed together, although this is often recommended. The light green foliage of the Day Lily is justly admired, but it is altogether coarser than the finely divided leaves of *Astilbe*. Moreover, the flowers of the Day Lily are strong and definite rather than light and fluffy. To combine these two plants is, to my mind, rather like laying a table with both pottery and cut-glass. Certainly there is room for *Hemerocallis* and *Astilbe* in the same bog garden, but divide them by rocks or ferns. And if you want a companion for the Day Lily, choose from among the cultivars of the Globe Flower or *Trollius europaeus*, whose yellow, white and orange blooms will mix well, while their globular shape will add an element of contrast.

And whatever selection you finally make among the many bog plants available, apply the same rule to them as to marginals. A series of large plantings of several plants is better by far than smaller groups of many. Resist the temptation to buy too wide a variety of plants. Having stocked the pond with water-lilies, marginals and bog plants, one can now turn one's attention to another dimension altogether: that of fish and animal life.

△ *Iris sibirica alba*

△ *Primula pulverulenta*

△ *Menyanthes trifoliata*

◁ *Astilbe* x Arendsii

7 FISH AND LIVESTOCK FOR THE POOL

There was a time when many ponds were referred to, especially by monks, as 'carp-pools'. For adjacent to many a monastery lay a pool well stocked with carp. Those fish often grew to a prodigious size, and when a meal was required, a monk or retainer simply netted a basket of fish. Refrigeration and improved transport put an end to the practice. But carp are still to be found in public and private lakes and ponds. The native Asian Carp, *Cyprinus carpio*, was introduced to Europe a long time ago. It averages about 30 to 40 cm. in length, but specimens 100 cm. long and 20 kilos in weight are not unknown. The Asian Carp is easily distinguished from the European Crucian Carp, *Carassius carassuis*, by having two barbels on each side of its upper jaw. Carp are extremely tame and will often cruise to the surface well within reach. I sometimes wonder how many of them may have provided a meal for some hungry poacher or tramp. There is no reason why one should not keep these friendly creatures in a largish pond except that their dark colour makes them rather inconspicuous. And they revel in rooting in the bottom of the pond and tearing up aquatic plants. So far as carp are concerned, the obvious choice for the ornamental pond is from the numerous varieties of goldfish (*Carassius auratus*). There are over one hundred

recognized types — all relatives of the humble carp.

Regardless of the varieties you choose, do select healthy fish. There is no difficulty in identifying them. A goldfish in the peak of condition will have an erect dorsal fin and his movement will be definite or vivacious. A sick fish will lie on the bottom, be motionless or almost so; and if he is not capable of swimming upright or keels over at all, then do not buy him. Presumably, you will transport your fish home in a polythene bag with water taken from the tank in the shop. This water may well be at quite a different temperature to the water in your pond. Fish are cold-blooded creatures which means they adapt their blood temperature to that of the surrounding water. They can survive in extremes of temperature, but they cannot adapt instantly from one extreme to another. So, rather than release your fish immediately into the pond, allow the polythene bag, with the neck open, to rest in the pond until the water in the bag is within a few degrees of the water in the pond. Then simply tip the bag over and release the fish. He should then dart off to hide in a clump of weed, under a rock, or if he is a larger specimen, he may begin exploring the pond immediately. And it is best not to introduce fish to a new pond until the underwater plants are growing well. This way one knows that the water is in fit condition for livestock.

TOP LEFT *Lionhead*, LEFT *Koi Carp*

Golden Orfe, Idus idus

The utter stillness of aquatic plants, especially the water-lily, in a way begs the constant motion of fish. If you have had the opportunity to become used to both in one pond, then you will almost certainly feel something is missing in a pond which has only one of these elements. And the relationship is not solely an aesthetic one. Fish may be chosen primarily for their ornamental value but they are also useful scavengers, protecting lilies from the onslaught of insects, among other creatures. They are worth including in a pond for this reason alone. And no fish is more beautiful nor more effective a scavenger than the Golden Orfe *(Idus idus)*, which is also available in a silver form. Long, slim fish that quickly grow up to 30 cm. and more, they tend to move in shoals especially when small and can whip and dart through the water at great speed. More important, they spend much

of their time at the surface, will readily take floating food including insects, and are on view frequently. Their characteristic flight through the water makes for a very satisfying contrast to the more languid, peaceful movements of the common goldfish which are, however, even more tame. Indeed it is not unusual for goldfish to become so tame that they will feed directly from the hand. Once this practice is established, as soon as you appear the fish will congregate at your feet. So too will Shubunkins or Calicoes which are varieties of goldfish, but which come in multicolours of red, black, brown, purple, white and most highly prized — and priced — of all, blue. They appear almost scaleless on account of the fact that their scales lack pigmentation. Shubunkins are also available in single colours and are very conspicuous fish. The sleek Hi Goi Carp are also available

106

in a variety of colours. They are clearly scaled and have two pairs of barbels.

Breeding grotesque and outlandish forms of goldfish has been brought to a fine art in Japan and America. Veiltails or Fantails have squat, fat bodies with long flowing tails usually in three sections and often as long as the head and the body put together, indeed sometimes longer. The Black Moor has, in addition to this kind of body and finnage, great bulbous, telescopic eyes. So highly developed has the finnage of these fish become that it is almost

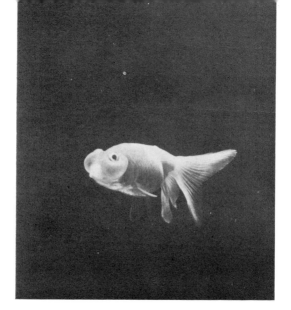

A Water Bubbli, or Bubble Eye

A fine specimen of Shubunkin

Hi Goi or Golden Carp

inoperative. Veiltails and Black Moors can only strut through the water like so many fat duchesses. This can be a problem if the fish is dependent upon food you throw into the water. Golden Orfe and the common goldfish easily outstrip them in speed, so special provision has to be made for them to be certain they do not starve to death. In a well-established pool with plenty of underwater plants all fish should do well enough grubbing for midge larvae, algae and other natural foods. Fantails and Black Moors are more susceptible to ailments than ordinary goldfish. In particular the air bladder, situated in the centre of their squat bodies, which controls their sense of balance, often gives rise to problems. If you are attracted by their long, flowing tails, but feel the Fantail is too ungainly or troublesome, then a compromise is possible in the Comet Goldfish. Their conspicuous tail fins are about a third of the length of their bodies, but short enough to be functional. They are very agile fish. All sorts of combinations of fancy characteristics have been bred into goldfish apart from elongated finnage. There is the Bubble Eye, and the Celestial Goldfish whose eyes are situated on top of its head. But to my mind the most grotesque of all is the Lionhead (p.104) which has large warts on its head not unlike the seeds of corn-on-the-cob. The more perfect the symmetry of the finnage of these goldfish, or the more highly developed their grotesqueries, the more expensive they come. In a pond, as opposed to an aquarium, where one is normally looking down at the fish from some distance, the finer points of symmetry are not apparent and one is as well off buying the cheaper, less perfectly shaped specimens. Symmetry is no indication whatever of the health of a fish, although it can be said that the more squat the body the more vulnerable is the fish to ailments.

Golden Orfe are not likely to breed in the average pond, but goldfish will breed readily during warm spring conditions. It is possible to buy goldfish in breeding pairs at extra cost. But this is hardly necessary as any five or six fish are almost certain to contain both sexes. Come the warm weather and the females or hen fish who are ready for spawning will develop fat, rotund bellies, while the males, or cock fish, who are ready for mating very often develop a pattern of small dots on their gill plates. A temperature of 15°-18°C. is favourable to spawning. The mating ritual consists of males frantically chasing a female round the pond, chivying and nudging her flanks encouraging her to spawn. Often this ritual goes on for hours at a time. Sometimes the female is cornered and almost forced out of the water. Occasionally her flanks can become torn from friction with rocks or the walls of the pond. This can lead to fungal infection, especially if the female is exhausted by so much attention. That, however, is the way with nature. In time the eggs are deposited usually on dense weed in shallow water and the male fertilizes them. Several spawnings may occur over a period of ten days. Depending upon the temperature the eggs will hatch in about three to five days. The fry are tiny, no larger than the head of a pin. It may be several months or even the following season before you spot them: thin, translucent initially and only a few millimetres in length. Fish are notorious cannibals and it is an advantage to have a shallow area in your pond in which the young can take refuge — in theory, if not always in practice, the larger fish will stick to the deeper areas. As they mature, some of the fry will take on the colour or mixed shades of their parents; others, unfortunately, will revert to the plain blackish-brown of their ancestors. Some may, in time, lose this dull colour in favour of red or yellow, but for a certain number black or olive brown will be their permanent colour. In commercial breeding, selection procedures are adopted and bright red hues are encouraged by the use of chemicals and high-temperature tanks. So far as pond fish are concerned, one has to rely on natural sunshine. But this does not mean preventing the fish from having adequate shelter in terms of rocks and weeds, which are essential to their well being. In an aquarium, artificial lighting may encourage fish to change colour, always provided, of course, that the individual fish has that potential. Again it is important to ensure that the fish have adequate cover should they want to use it.

Goldfish rarely suffer from underfeeding but are vulnerable to being fed too much too often. In winter, fish in an outdoor pool hibernate, hidden among the weeds, emerging only during warm, sunny spells. They require no feeding at all during this time and any food they look for can easily be found amongst the weeds. In summer, in addition to fish pellets and other patent foods, fish are grateful for an occasional diet of chopped worms, if you can bear to chop them, *Daphnia* and a portion of a hard-boiled egg that has been very thoroughly chopped up or minced. But whatever you feed your fish, never give them more than they can consume within about fifteen minutes. If food is left lying around, not only will it discolour and possibly pollute the pond (boiled egg is a particular danger), but it is a sure indication that the fish are being overfed. In a well-planted pool, the base of which is almost covered with oxygenators, feeding is hardly necessary at all. So you can limit the expense of buying fish food to those occasions when you want to bring the fish up to the surface and close to view, and to tame them. Feeding in spring may encourage your fish to breed; while in autumn it should build up their strength for hibernation. Of particular value to fish fry are the minute organisms known as infusoria associated with decaying vegetable matter. Infusoria can be prepared by taking a little water from the pond in a jar and suspending

in it a bruised and rotting lettuce leaf. Spinach leaves, lentils, the dead leaves of water plants and even a banana skin will serve the same purpose. Best results are likely to be obtained if the water temperature is around 22°C. or above. After a few days you can judge whether infusorians are present by holding the container up to the light. The water should appear as if filled with a greyish-white dust. These are the infusorians. Simply tip the contents of the container into the pool, preferably at roughly the same temperature as the pool water, to prevent killing the culture.

To have seen the Koi Carp (p.104) is to have seen the most magnificent of all pond fish. Unlike Shubunkins, their scales are very obvious and pronounced and their colours are even more striking, especially the golden form. There is no more brightly coloured ornamental fish available. The golden form is truly the colour of gold, not merely a shade of yellow. And Koi are not simply tame. They are fearless. Dip your fingers in the water and immediately you can expect your hand to be surrounded by Koi, all clamouring and jockeying for position in the expectation of tit-bits. They grow to great sizes, and a pond containing five or ten Koi, each weighing upwards of two kilos, is an unrivalled sight. You could, however, buy a three-piece suit for the price of one such fish, and still have change in your pocket. Better to begin with small fish and feed them up. But that is one of the drawbacks of these beautiful fish. They have large appetites and require a substantial diet that might include *Tubifex, Daphnia,* pelleted food and small earthworms. They are by nature bottom feeders and have the habit of churning up the soil in baskets or on the bottom of the pool and uprooting aquatic plants. It has to be said that water-lilies and Koi are not wholly compatible, unless your pond is a large one. And they like deep, well-oxygenated water. A waterfall would be an obvious advantage.

Green and Golden Tench (*Tinca tinca*) will

live in harmony with goldfish and are often recommended for ponds on account of the fact that they are scavenger fish, eating detritus and grubbing around in the bottom of the pool. The fact that they can survive in water with a low oxygen content makes them easy to keep. But being bottom feeders they are rarely seen in a pond which has an adequate planting of weeds; and their value in mopping up dead snails and keeping the pond clean is probably over-estimated. Similarly, the little Bitterling *(Rhodeus amarus)*, 8 or 9 cm. long, and the Gudgeon *(Gobio gobio)* are not likely to be seen or noticed. On the other hand a small shoal of Minnow *(Phoxinus phoxinus)* is an attractive feature. True, their colour is non-descript, but their activities, flitting around, suddenly seen in one space only to disappear into a clump of weeds and reappear somewhere else, make them worth keeping. Apparently their habit of scattering — as opposed to staying together — in the face of danger, is a tactic for survival. It is believed that a predator is unable to concentrate his attention on one particular minnow when a shoal scatters in all directions.

And the Stickleback *(Gasterosteus aculeatus)* is certainly worth including, not only for its subtle colouring of red and blue lines along the flank, but also for its characteristic movement and above all for its unusual life-style. The stickleback always appears as a very self-possessed little fish, thrusting itself through the water at great speed and then pulling up sharply to remain motionless until it gets it into its head to take off again, and again pulling up dead as if attached to some miniature and invisible braking system. At mating time, usually from early spring until midsummer, the female loses her greeny black colour for a shade of yellow; and the male's flank takes on a strong red hue, his back a bright green and his eyes become electric blue. He then sets about collecting small pieces of vegetation which he glues together in some nook, and this serves as a nest. The glue is secreted from the kidneys. An elaborate courtship follows during which the female or females

RIGHT *The Great Pond Snail, Limnaea stagnalis. Note the egg rope laid by another snail being carried on its back.*

BELOW LEFT *The Catfish is as ferocious as it looks. Although they are often sold by aquarists, on no account introduce them to a pond containing other fish.*

are enticed into his parlour to lay their eggs. Once the nest is full of eggs, the female stickleback has no further duties. The male takes charge of the eggs, fertilizes them of course, aerates the water in their vicinity by vibrating his fins, and protects them and the hatched fry until they are old enough to fend for themselves. Any young stickleback who tries to leave the nest before father approves is taken in father's mouth and thrust back into the nest. Sticklebacks are not, contrary to what is sometimes said, a danger to other species of fish. They keep their aggression for defending their territory against other sticklebacks. The same is certainly not the case with the ferocious catfish (members of the genus *Corydoras* are the ones commonly kept in aquariums) who will eat all before it. And under no circumstances should the Brown Trout *(Salmo trutta),* the Common Perch *(Perca fluviatilis)* or the Pike *(Esox lucius)* be introduced into ponds which contain goldfish.

About introducing such predatory fish with goldfish there is no debate at all. Trout, perch and pike will devour the goldfish. About introducing snails and mussels, opinion is somewhat divided. If your interest in a pond embraces the creatures it can support as much as the plants, then snails in their various shapes and colours, their behaviour and egg capsules, will undoubtedly add to that interest. Snails are valuable in that they eat decaying vegetable

matter and perhaps serve a purpose in keeping the pond free of pollution. Not all of them, however, limit themselves to decaying matter. The Great Pond Snail, *Limnaea stagnalis,* is very partial to Frogbit, oxygenating plants and the leaves of water-lilies, especially the smaller plants. This snail can be easily recognized by its conical shell 5-6 cm. high. Keeping it out of the pond entirely is almost impossible. *Limnaea* are hermaphrodite or bisexual. This means that not only can a 'male' and 'female' reverse their roles at will — they

The Three-spined Stickleback, Gasterosteus aculeatus

111

Great Ramshorn Snail, Planorbis corneus, on the water surface, showing its tentacles and siphon.

often do during courtship, especially if two snails are joined by a third — but a single snail can fertilize its own eggs. The implication is obvious. If one *Limnaea* gets into your pond, it can quickly raise a colony, laying egg capsules as long as itself and containing up to 300 eggs. *Limnaea* nearly always succeed in entering new ponds, either the snail or its eggs being carried in surreptitiously on aquatics or marginals. But there is no need to attempt to eradicate them, even if that were possible; keeping down their numbers will solve any problems. The Ramshorn Snails are often recommended for ornamental ponds because they do not eat lily leaves and the like. They have shells which are not conical like *Limnaea*, but are flat. It is worth introducing the Great Ramshorn, *Planorbis corneus*, a red-blooded snail about 35 mm. wide, or its more decorative relation, *Planorbis corneus rubra* which has reddish rather than a black or brownish shell. Under suitable conditions these snails can breed at a prolific rate while under others they may not succeed in breeding at all. One can only try introducing a few and seeing if your pond has the right conditions.

Mussels too are particular about their environment. They require the presence of mud. Where plants are rooted directly in the soil in the base of the pond the mussel offers a hazard. When it moves round it tends to uproot oxygenators in its path. (Their movement can

be curtailed by building up a circular wall of stones which they will be unable to cross.) In their favour it can be said that a mussel continually siphons water while feeding off the algae. In this way a few mussels can be a great help in keeping a pond clear. The contention that a dead mussel offers a serious threat of pollution is probably exaggerated, unless one is talking about a sink pond or the like. But if you want to introduce mussels into your pond, you would be well advised to introduce one species only. That is the Zebra Mussel, *Dreissena polymorpha*, which is about 2 to 4 cm. long and is banded in two shades of brown. The larvae of this mussel do not attach themselves as parasites on passing fish as some mussels do; and the mature Zebra Mussel is not liable to uproot plants.

No risk is attached to the introduction of frogs. And no creature, to my way of thinking, adds a greater sense of homeliness to the garden pool. Their appearance in the pool every spring to breed, the pleasant, often frenetic activities of the tadpoles, the occasional hopping and prancing of the young frogs when disturbed in the undergrowth, all add to the sense of the pond as a centre of life. But not everyone will agree. About the Common Frog *(Rana temporaria)*, the Edible Frog *(Rana esculenta)* or the Marsh Frog *(Rana ridibunda)* most people have a very decided opinion. They are found either delightful or repulsive. Their shiny skins in muted colours, their squat bodies and sad liquid eyes are not found equally appealing by everyone. If you find nothing especially attractive about these creatures, tolerate one of the species for its usefulness in eating pests.

In Britain, the frog population has been drastically reduced due to the drainage of areas of marshy ground during agricultural and urban reclamation. School biology lessons have made children everywhere familiar with frogs, and in North America the common species is the Leopard Frog *(Rana pipiens)*.

The Common Toad – Bufo bufo

This versatile frog can stand extremes of temperature and is found as far north as Canada and as far south as Mexico. As the name would imply, all Leopard Frogs are heavily blotched or spotted, but their overall colouring varies from grey through green to brown. The Leopard Frog grows to about 12 cm. in length and like the massive American Bullfrog *(Rana catesbeiana),* 20 cm. long with legs up to 25 cm., it is renowned for its prodigious jumping ability. A good specimen of Leopard or Bullfrog in energetic mood can leap a distance of 1.4 m. and more. The Bullfrog has the unusual characteristic of guarding its tadpoles which will cluster round the parent for safety. Such cautious behaviour is probably necessary as the tadpoles may remain as tadpoles for up to three years, and that is a vulnerable stage in a frog's life. Adult Bullfrogs will spend their lives in or close to still water, unlike the Wood Frog *(Rana sylvatica)* which favours damp woodland areas, except when visiting ponds in spring to breed. It grows to little more than 8 cm. in length and is widely distributed through the south-eastern states of America to as far north as Alaska. The colouring of the Wood Frog is very variable, ranging from brown, black and yellow to a pinkish colour. Obviously, the Wood Frog is suited primarily to ponds with a natural woodland setting, and the Bullfrog is rather too large for the small garden pond.

Where space and food supply may be limited, a more congenial species and one common to ponds and streams in the north-eastern states is the Green Frog *(Rana clamitans melanota)* which may grow to no more than 8-10 cm. Despite its name it can be brown as well as green and is blotched. An even smaller version, the so-called Bronze Frog *(R. clamitans clamitans),* is found further south.

The American Toad *(Bufo americanus)* deserves respect for its voracious appetite for mosquitoes; while the Common Toad *(Bufo bufo)* and the Natterjack *(Bufo calamita),* both native to Europe, have a useful diet consisting

The Common Newt – Triturus vulgaris

113

of caterpillars, beetles and other pests. So does the Common or Smooth Newt, *Triturus vulgaris* 6-8 cm. long and widely distributed; and the Palmate Newt, *Triturus helveticus*, which is widespread in Western Europe but less easy to find. The hind feet of the male Palmate are webbed and his tail ends in a thin filament. The Great Crested Newt, *Triturus cristatus*, is the largest European species, growing 12-16 cm. long. It has a rather warty appearance. Secretive, agile creatures, newts come to the pond to breed in spring or summer, as do toads. The Great Crested Newt is the only newt which may remain in the pool to hibernate during the winter. The others leave after breeding and may roam far and wide. They are most likely to be seen in hot weather when they leave their secret haunts in water to sunbathe. There can hardly be a child who is not enthralled by their appearance, especially in spring when the males are at their most colourful. All newts shed their skins from time to time, rather in the manner of snakes but with greater ease. Sometimes an entire transparent coat is to be seen floating in the water, that is, if the newt has not devoured it. Newts can sometimes be caught by drawing a worm on the end of a piece of string through the water of a wild pond. Often a newt will hold on to the worm and it can then be brought to the bank. Newts make excellent aquarium pets where their mating ritual can be observed and the females' habit of folding the leaves of submerged water plants over each individual egg can be watched. They are best returned to the outdoor pond or to the wild in mid-summer. In America, the Japanese newt, *Cynops pyrrhogaster*, has become a popular pet.

If you intend keeping Veiltails and Black Moors an aquarium is almost essential. These delicate fish (like many other hybrids) require comparatively high temperatures and should be over-wintered in an indoor aquarium. You could also bring in the young fry of the gold-

fish as a means of separating them from their predatory elders. And there is the added advantage that with an aquarium there is no closed season. Instead of your fish hibernating, hidden in the depth of the pool, you can enjoy their graceful lives and those of many other creatures in your own house during the winter, and at close quarters.

A typical plastic moulded aquarium

8

KEEPING
A WINTER AQUARIUM

Instant aquariums, like instant pools, are easy to come by. Transparent plastic models, either produced as a single piece from a mould or composed of five separate sheets, are the most common aquariums. Plastic tanks do have the disadvantage, however, of scratching rather easily, and this is a serious disadvantage because algae will inevitably grow on the inside surfaces of the tank and these must be constantly scraped clean. To be sure, a plastic aquarium can, with care, be cleaned without scratching. But the risk is always there. By comparison a glass aquarium can be cleaned with impunity; and glass aquariums can be made up at home much more easily than you might imagine. And of course a home-made tank means a significant saving on cost.

A glass merchant will supply five sheets of glass cut to the required sizes, and preferably with the top edges smoothed off (you can then put your hand into the tank without risk of grazing your wrist). Do explain to the glass cutter the purpose for which you intend using the glass. He should then appreciate that the sides and the base must fit together absolutely perfectly. And the tank should be designed so that the base sits *within* the four sides, not so that the sides sit upon the base. This is the way to make the most waterproof and permanent of joints. Nothing else is required but a tube of silicone rubber glue which a fish stockist will supply. This should be

smeared thoroughly over all the edges that are to be joined together. Match the four sides to the base — you may find four hands better than two for this operation — make sure the joints are perfectly aligned, then hold the lot together with sticky tape for about eight hours or until the glue has set. Silicone rubber, you will find, retains a high degree of flexibility, but the joints will be remarkably strong, as indeed they must. Ten litres of water weighs ten kilos, and yet this film of glue can well withstand the pressure that water exerts and more. The point to watch in applying the glue is that it is spread over the entire length of each surface to be joined. If this is done the tank will be quite free of leaks.

A cover for the tank will cut down on the amount of dust entering the water. It also serves a useful purpose in providing a ceiling to which lights can be attached. More important, if you intend keeping newts, a cover is essential to prevent them scrambling out of the tank. Plastic aquariums are usually supplied with plastic covers. If you have made your own tank, then plywood is probably the simplest material from which to make one. It need only extend beyond the sides of the tank by a few centimetres, but I would ensure that it was slightly raised over the tank to allow the free passage of air. A few wooden slats glued across the underside of the cover will achieve this. And a 'lip' of wood the whole

115

A glass aquarium made with five sheets of glass. Note how the cover is supported by wooden laths to allow the free passage of air.

way round the cover will hide the slats from view. It will also conceal whatever form of lighting you intend to use. Tubular fluorescent lights are the most suitable. They give off little heat which is an advantage and are economic in use. And since tubular lights are designed to be set in brackets there is no problem about attaching them to the cover. A single tube is normally quite sufficient. Remember to site it not down the middle of the cover, but towards the front. Positioned so, the illumination will be spread over the whole tank and not part of it; and fish swimming in the foreground will not be turned into silhouettes.

Whatever your confidence in your handiwork, common sense suggests you test your new aquarium either out of doors or in the kitchen sink. Once satisfied that it holds water right up to the top, empty it and place it on its permanent site. And permanent the site must be. The tank, if it is any size at all, cannot be moved again until it is emptied. Do bear in mind that the shelf of a bookcase may be sturdy enough for large, heavy books but not for a large volume of water. A sagging shelf can have disastrous consequences. And if the tank receives direct sunlight, it is imperative that you provide some form of shield or shelter for the fish. Small rocks are suitable and will add to the naturalness of your tank. Few aquarists, incidentally, would

allow their tanks to get direct sun unless they were trying to change the colour of their fish. Rapid changes in temperature can be detrimental and sunlight encourages growth of algae. One other point is worth bearing in mind when siting an aquarium. Make sure you can get your arm over the top of the tank easily and without obstructions such as a higher shelf or an alcove ceiling that is too low. Cleaning a tank, introducing or removing fish, weeds, rocks or whatever, can be accomplished in minutes when access is free; otherwise you will quickly find it becomes a laborious chore.

Some aquarists favour growing oxygenating plants in a few centimetres of soil spread over the base of the tank, over which in turn a layer of gravel or sand is laid to prevent the fish muddying the water. Others are content to plant the oxygenators directly into sand or gravel. If you opt for using soil, obtain a light, poor-quality loam as free from decaying leaves and organic matter as possible. Sand used either on its own or as a protective layer has a slight advantage over gravel. Particles of food and detritus cannot slip so easily between grains of sand as between nuggets of gravel. Fish and snails are then more likely to consume such items and there is less chance of pollution. Make sure the sand or gravel you use is quite free of soil or sediment. It should be sieved and washed clean.

If you have a seasoned pond, then I would

Mirror carp, Cyprinus carpio, with a Nymphaea in an aquarium.

fill up the aquarium with water taken from it. Failing that, rain water from an unpolluted rain barrel can be used. Be quite certain, however, that the barrel did not originally contain oil or chemicals. If neither of these sources of water is available then tap water must be used; letting it 'settle' for a few days before bringing in the fish may help to remove chlorine in the water. When filling the tank there is a simple way to avoid churning up the soil. Place a bowl on the bottom of the tank. Fill this with water and allow it to overflow slowly on to the surrounding sand and soil. The bowl can be removed once the tank is partially filled. A saving of work and trouble is to be made by planting your oxygenators in miniature flower pots — thumb pots as they are sometimes called — which can be buried a centimetre or less below the surface of the gravel or sand. An excellent practice is to have a number of these tiny pots in the outdoor pool, so that one has well-established, vigorous plants which can be brought in to serve the aquarium as required. Fish are partial to nibbling underwater foliage and will often divest a plant of all leaves, even when fish flakes or whatever are provided.

Any of the oxygenating plants that you are using in the outdoor pond are suitable for the aquarium, with the exception of *Callitriche stagnalis* which prefers to be left out in the cold. *Elodea* is often used in aquariums. Fish seem to find its leaves succulent, but as there is always a plentiful supply of *Elodea* in any pond in which it is kept, there is no problem about replenishing it. The Tape Grass, *Vallisneria spiralis,* and Curled Pondweed, *Potamogeton crispus,* are somewhat tougher and will last longer in the aquarium; and they are attractive in their own right. The oxygen exchange between the surface of the water and the surrounding air (when there is adequate space between the cover and the sides of the tank), and the activities of the oxygenating plants will satisfy the needs of a few fish. As a guide, for every centimetre of fish (excluding tail)

one needs about 20 sq. cm. of water surface. So a tank 36 x 25 cm. could support 45 cm. of fish. Far more satisfactory, however, is the practice of aerating the water by means of a miniature electric pump. Stocking rates can be doubled and the amount of electricity these pumps use is negligible. One end of a piece of plastic tubing is connected to the pump and the other end to an 'aerator stone' which gives off myriads of air bubbles when placed in the aquarium. As well as raising the oxygen content of the water, carbon dioxide and other noxious gases are forced out of the water. Even better than the aerator stone is the combination of filter and aerator. This consists of a plastic container with holes or slits along its top surface. Fibreglass padding is tucked into this container, sometimes with grains of charcoal underneath to act as a freshener. Air from the pump is circulated in the container and emerges in a series of bubbles. At the same time, the fibreglass filters out algae blooms, detritus and other waste matter, and when you scrape off the algae deposit from the sides of the tank, the filter will rapidly absorb what

Bladderwort, which traps and digests minute organisms, is an interesting plant for the aquarium.

A typical plastic filter-aerator.   119

A female Great Crested Newt, Triturus cristatus, wrapping a leaf around a newly-laid egg.

you have not collected in a fine net. An old razor blade makes the best kind of scraper for glass tanks but should never be used for plastic ones. The safest material with which to scrape algae off plastic is another piece of plastic, anything harder will almost certainly leave unsightly scratches.

When feeding your fish, turn off the pump so that food will not be absorbed by the filter container. If you have judged the amount of food your fish require, then there should be none left over. Fish are being adequately fed if they show enthusiasm for food without being frantic. They are most certainly being overfed if they show a take-it-or-leave-it attitude to newly introduced food, or leave large quantities of it untouched. And it is worth repeating that overfed fish become increasingly susceptible to ailments. Mature fish and fry must be kept apart. Either place them in separate tanks or use a dividing glass screen running lengthwise in one aquarium. A partition, incidentally, is sometimes used to prevent fish eating plants which are placed behind the screen as a background decoration. But cleaning a glass partition is troublesome. It tends to fall down or you cannot get your hands into the corners. Fish all too easily get into the wrong section. I would prefer to use two tanks where adult fish and fry are concerned.

If you want to keep newts to watch their courtship rituals and the antics of their little wriggling tadpoles, then they must be kept apart from fish. Newts will prey on small fish, and the Great Crested Newt is not above attack-ing its smaller cousins and its own young. And the tadpoles of frogs are liable to be preyed upon by both newts and fish, and not a few water insects as well. A garden pond, if one could only observe its depths, is like a watery Coliseum where the cycle of life is maintained by one creature preying off another.

If you are keeping only adult goldfish in the aquarium, and not fry, you can safely introduce a larger number of other creatures as well. Try sweeping your pond with a net and you should come up with a variety of life. *Tubifex tubifex* worms live with one end buried in mud and the other waving round above the level of the soil. They are easily recognized by being bright red. Fish are fond of them. You might be able to get hold of a Caddis larvae or two. They construct protective cases composed of small pieces of wood, grains of sand and other bits of material to be found on the bed of rivers and ponds. If you push the larva out of its case with the head of a pin, you will have the opportunity of watching the process of case-building in the aquarium. The larva will not succeed in making quite as fine a case the second time round; nevertheless the process is a fascinating one to watch. Make sure the naked larva has access to some small twigs, leaves and sand. A sweep of your net through dense weed should produce a leech or two, which will snake through the aquarium at high speed. They are rather repulsive creatures though. I would prefer to find in my net some freshwater shrimps. I have always liked the way they busy themselves at the bottom of the aquarium, wandering around in their search for food. A Backswimmer or Water Boatman *(Notonecta glauca)* can be safely introduced if your goldfish are large, otherwise it is not worth the risk. A Water Boatman can pierce small prey with its powerful mouth, killing it at a single stab; and it is quite capable of giving your finger a nasty prick. The Water Boatman normally swims on its back with a characteristic jerky movement. When it dives, it carries down a store of air which adheres to the bristles on its body. You should notice the silvery appearance this gives the Water Boatman under water. Being lighter than water, it usually holds on to a piece of weed as an anchor when submerged. It would also be worth introducing some *Daphnia magna* or Water Fleas, which are quite tiny, about 5 mm. You can encourage their generation by steeping a little manure and decaying leaves in a bowl of water in the vicinity of your pond or wherever they are present. *Daphnia* should have some effect on the algae blooms in your aquarium since they feed off them, and the fish will in turn enjoy a meal of *Daphnia*.

And one should certainly include a number of snails. They too will feed off algae and detritus as well. Snails can live for long periods under water, but every now and again you will see them rise to the surface to take in air. Quite often you will see the curious sight of snails walking along the under-surface of the water, seemingly gripping the 'skin' of water formed by surface tension. Touch a snail in this position and it will instantly sink to the bottom like a stone. This is not because the snail has let go of the skin of water, but because it has quickly expelled the air from its lungs when it sensed danger. Sometimes you may find the snail fearless, and it simply bobs up and down in the water as you push it with your finger. Having expelled air to sink, it can rise again by extending its body, so reducing the density of its body weight.

All these creatures and many more can be kept in an aquarium, and you might wonder if the aquarium could not become a miniature pond in which water-lilies, marginals and floating plants might not also be kept. In theory at least it is possible; in practice only partially so. The problem is that the amount of sunlight water-lilies and many marginals need, inevitably means a huge build-up of algae. Examine the walls of your outdoor pond and even though the water may be crystal clear, you will see algae blooms over virtually every centimetre of concrete or liner. An indoor conservatory pond can, of course, be built as easily as an outdoor one. It is the transparent sides of the aquarium that pose the problem.

If you want to try water-lilies indoors, they must have all the light possible. Miniature water-lilies are the obvious choice for small tanks (remember that snails are partial to their leaves). Among the floating plants, the duckweeds, Frogbit and Water Lettuce (given a high enough temperature) should do well in your aquarium. The Water Hyacinth is obviously worth trying. It will flower in a warm room with plenty of sunshine. The Water Soldier is likely to be too big and cumbersome for most indoor tanks and prefers to be outdoors. The Lemnas are excellent for the small tank, as they make very pretty surface decorations. In particular, the fronds of the Ivy Duckweed appear altogether more dainty and attractive when viewed at close quarters. Indeed all plants and livestock will probably take on a different perspective in the indoor tank. Begin an aquarium and you may wonder if you ever *really* looked at all those plants and fish before.

Having stocked your pond with plant and animal life you may well wonder: what are the problems and snags associated with water gardening?

9 PITFALLS, PROBLEMS AND POND CARE

Cracks and leaks

If you were to ask ten water gardeners what they considered to be the worst problem associated with ponds, you would probably receive but one single answer from all ten. A pond that leaks constitutes the worst problem.

No water, obviously, means no pond. Fortunately, leaks are rarely so severe as to leave a pond empty. But any leakage that is discernible creates problems. The constant topping up of the water level with the garden hose is not only an added chore, but also adds unnecessarily to the chemical content of the water upon which algae thrive. Tap water will also tend to chill the water in the pond which in turn will reduce the vigour of the water-lilies and they may not bloom so freely. Evaporation during the hot days of summer is bound to lower the water level to some extent, and topping up cannot be avoided entirely. Leakage may increase the amount of topping up to an unsatisfactory degree. And finally, a leaking pond often means the inconvenience of having an area of lawn or pathway which is constantly soggy.

Concrete ponds can develop leaks for a number of reasons, all but one of which can be avoided during the course of construction.

The common heron, a beautiful sight on a river or estuary, a dreadful sight by a pond.

Only fresh and clean materials should be used. If there are any lumps in the cement these should quickly turn to powder when lightly rubbed between the fingers. If they are in any way hard, then the bag of cement should be rejected; there should be no lumps of cement in the mix. In the pond in which the cement, sand and aggregate have not been well mixed, soft, porous areas are bound to develop quickly. These areas will be immediately obvious by their pitted appearance and by the fact that they become powdery when given a sharp tap. This problem should never arise. It cannot be over-stressed: mix the ingredients dry, break down any lumps of sand or cement that form, and mix the lot *thoroughly*. And when placing the concrete in the site, do not throw it in but shovel it in with some care, otherwise the ingredients may tend to separate. Some writers recommend giving the pond a facing of cement and sand in the ratio 1:3. The only reason for doing this is to provide the pond with a smoother finish. But the interior surfaces become virtually invisible once the pond has been filled with water and planted, so I do not see much point in finishing the pond in this way. It should certainly not be carried out with the intention of making the pond waterproof. The original concreting should do that. It is perhaps worth mentioning, since I know a case in point, that if you come across a massive boulder while excavating the site, it must either be removed or concreted right over (to the required thickness). It is no use concreting around such an obstacle because concrete and rock will not form a watertight bond.

Assuming that you have carried out the concreting properly, the walls are of uniform thickness, the reinforcing wire is thoroughly embedded in the base and walls, and the foundation is perfectly stable, then the only other reason as to why your pond might crack lies in the formation of ice in winter. If you live in a climate in which several centimetres of ice is the norm, then I would be inclined to make the walls of the pond somewhat thicker than 15 cm. This is particularly important if the walls of the pond are perpendicular. Even a slight slant outwards offers a considerable safeguard against cracking. And the pressure of the ice can be reduced further by keeping a rubber tyre or a few lengths of soft wood in the pond during severe weather.

If your pond does develop a crack there are few courses of action you can take. If it is no more than a hairline crack, clean the area surrounding it with a wire brush and apply a coat of bitumen paint or of rapid-hardening patent cement. The application, in either case, should not be confined to the crack but spread a fair distance around it as well. In many cases a waterproof join will result but there is no certainty about it. In the case of large or widespread cracks the simplest remedy is to install a liner over the concrete, having first removed any sharp projections. Otherwise there is nothing for it but to re-concrete the entire site. There is no need to remove the old concrete, except, of course, the reconstituted pond will be smaller in area by the additional thickness of the new walls and base.

Liner ponds will not crack, but they are probably more vulnerable to children who enjoy 'messing about with water'. And what child does not enjoy playing beside, and given the chance, in water? A broken glass, a garden fork, not to mention the innumerable knick knacks with which children play, are all a potential means of puncturing the skin of Butyl rubber or PVC. To be sure, these materials can take a certain amount of prodding and misuse, nevertheless the possibility of a puncture is always present. Puncturing may also occur if any sharp stones or the like are not removed from the foundation before the liner is placed in position. Land movement also offers a hazard: sharp stones may become exposed which had been concealed before. A subsidence of soil in the base or even the sides may leave a hollow beneath the liner and should someone step into the hollow then the liner may be forced to stretch beyond its elastic capability and a tear is inevitable. And the walls of the liner should not be placed under too much tension. Make certain the liner is lying smoothly over the *entire* base and fitting snugly into the corners. When making a raised pond this point should be particularly noted, as the temptation is to raise up the liner a little so that the sides are taut. Repairs to Butyl rubber and PVC are permanent, but do not underestimate the trouble involved in finding and repairing a leak. It requires emptying, cleaning and drying out the pond, and it may involve examining the liner centimetre by centimetre until the leak is located. Perhaps the old saying: 'prevention is better than cure' was concocted by an old pond builder!

In hot weather, the occasional topping up of the pond should not greatly increase the algae growth. But there is one situation where, regardless of the topping up involved or the number of oxygenators present, algae seem to thrive at a high level. The reason for this — all else being equal — is the ratio between the surface area of the pond and its volume. If the pond is very shallow in relation to its surface area then there is proportionately little water to absorb the light and heat and algae may thrive. The worst shape for a pond is a saucer shape: broad, gently curving sides and little depth. Ponds that are very shallow are unsatisfactory for other reasons too. The shallower the pond the more rapidly will the water change temperature. Neither water-lilies nor fish care for that. Moreover, in winter, fish like to hibernate at a reasonable depth, out of the way of ice and prey. Floating pond heaters are now available which will keep an area of water free of ice during cold weather. The idea is that toxic gases can thus escape from the water and oxygen enter it. However, fish use very little oxygen while

hibernating, and provided your pond is free of dead leaves and is of a reasonable depth, there is no need of such mollycoddling. Incidentally, never crack ice: the vibration can seriously affect your fish's balancing mechanism. It is safer to melt it with water from a hot kettle if you must. Snow over ice may be more of a problem than the ice itself. If light is completely excluded from the pond over a long period, it is possible that the oxygenating plants will die off. Brushing the snow off a section of the pond should remove this risk.

Plant ailments

So much for the actual pond; water-lilies and marginal plants are susceptible to few ailments. Nymphaeas may sometimes suffer from a fungus disease of the genus *Cercosporae*. This is comparatively rare, but when the fungus is present, spots will develop on the leaves which became dry and crumpled. A light spraying of Bordeaux mixture, applied every other day at half the strength directed for other plants, is the only remedy. The affected leaves should, of course, be removed. But do not mistake the natural decay of leaves for this fungus. If healthy leaves are rising to the surface and developing as others are dying off, then this is only evidence of the natural cycle of events. And, of course, once autumn frosts have arrived you can expect the Nymphaeas to die back quickly.

A peculiarity of some water-lilies is the phenomenon known as fasciation. An individual plant may grow and flower normally for a number of years. Then, for no apparent reason, it ceases to bloom and instead of producing leaves of usual size, it throws up a much larger number of tiny leaves. If you lift the plant you will discover, instead of just a few separate and well-defined growing points, a jungle of leaves and shoots growing all over the tuber. Fasciation is rare, but when it occurs there is only one solution. Remove any eyes or shoots that appear normal. These can be planted and should grow into ordinary tubers which will flower and produce leaves of the usual size. The original tuber can be discarded.

Reverting to type is a tendency that you may notice with some of your variegated marginals. In amongst the variegated foliage plain green stems may develop. Given time, the whole plant may revert to the plain colour of its ancestors and you will have lost the variegated species with which you began. The only thing you can do is cut out the plain stems as they arise and hope that the rest of the plant will remain true to type. The fact that the variegation on the leaves of *Iris pseudacorus variegatus,* for example, may lose some of their lustre, the green and bright creamy stems taking on a duller appearance at the end of summer, is not evidence of reverting to type, but only of the ageing process of the leaves. Should any straight leaves appear on *Juncus effusus spiralis,* they also should be ruthlessly cut out.

Plant pests

Much more of a nuisance than either of those problems are the pests which attack the leaves and tubers of water-lilies. Among these can be included: aphids, especially the reddish-black one, the Water-lily Aphis, *Rhopalosiphum nymphaeae;* the larva of Caddis flies, *Trichoptera,* and of the Brown China Marks Moth, *Nymphula nymphaeata.* Aphids lay their eggs on the leaves of water-lilies and the larvae feed off the leaves. The China Marks Moths lay their eggs near the edge of leaves or underneath them and the larvae are quite capable of destroying the foliage. The larvae of the Caddis fly, in its protective suit of armour, crawls about the bottom of the pond and can sometimes damage the tubers of water-lilies and their buds. To say as much about these pests is to conjure up a picture

ABOVE LEFT *The Brown China Marks Moth, Nymphula nymphaeta, has white wings with brown markings. The caterpillar of this moth builds for itself a watertight case made of leaf fragments and silk. The case is attached to the underside of leaves floating in the water. During the winter the caterpillar hibernates but in spring it feeds hungrily off adjacent vegetation.*

LEFT *This Nymphaea leaf clearly illustrates the kind of damage a severe infestation of the larvae of the Brown China Marks Moth and other insects can do. A certain amount of puncturing of leaves is usual, but when fish are present it is unlikely to reach this state.*

125

Caddis larva (Phryganea species) emerging from its case.

The Caddis larva (Limnephilus species) case BELOW is made of shells, tiny stones or grit and pieces of wood. Contrary to what is sometimes claimed, it is not possible to identify species from the materials which make up the protective cases. Certain species do show general preferences in choosing their materials. This case is about 25 mm. long.

of a pond ravaged and denuded. The extent of the problem is very much a matter of luck. These insects may be quite rare in one area and quite common in another. But the remedies are both simple and effective. The most important one is fish; have your pond well-stocked with young, vigorous goldfish and Golden Orfe, and they will feed readily off these insects and their larvae. The leaves of water-lilies often rise well clear of the surface and the upper portion of all floating leaves will, of course, be out of the reach of the fish. So you can aid the fish in two ways. Spraying the leaves with a firm jet of water is one way: the insects are forced into the water. The other is to spread a net over the lily leaves and submerge them by holding down the net with weights. Placing plants in a bath of Derris is sometimes recommended. But the cure may prove worse than the pests. Derris is highly toxic to fish and unless all traces of the insecticide are washed off the plants before returning them to the pond, you may find yourself minus your fish stock. I would use such a measure only in the most extreme of cases. Where aphids are a particular problem, cut back the dead foliage of marginals hard and burn it. The adult insects hibernate in the hollow stems of waterside plants. Finally, the Freshwater Snail, *Limnaea stagnalis*, will often develop a taste for leaves and sometimes buds. However, given the choice, this snail prefers the head of a lettuce or a cabbage stump to water-lilies. Place one or two of these plants in the water on a few successive nights and simply remove the snails attached to them. Surplus snails are quickly eradicated in this way.

As regards floating plants — the Water Soldier and Frogbit in particular — pond owners are sometimes baffled by the fact that they had a plentiful supply in one season only to find that they have none in the next. What had happened? It is possible that the plants simply rotted away at the end of the summer.

But the owner's own conscientiousness may have been his undoing. The Frogbit spends the winter months as small, insignificant buds resting on or immersed in the mud on the bottom of the pool. Similarly, the Water Soldier may only survive the winter in the form of little bulblets which grew and separated from the mature plant in summer. In cleaning out a pond in autumn one can unwittingly throw out these plants. It is not a bad idea to collect them before they sink to the bottom and transfer them to a jar of water. The same can be done with the seeds of *Trapa natans*, the Water Chestnut (but it will hardly ever set seed in the British Isles or Ireland).

Cleaning the pond

Talking of cleaning a pond, how thorough should one be? Even if you grow all your plants in baskets, it is inevitable that the base of the pond will, in a short time, receive a layer of mud and debris and probably small stones. In the case of liner pools the stones are worth removing for fear of damage. But a certain amount of mud is unavoidable and there is no point in continually removing it. Pond maintenance means preventing pollution above anything else. The decay and putrefaction of water plants and the leaves from nearby trees, especially in a small shallow pond, can destroy the quality of the water and can prove fatal to fish. Any sign of an oily sheen on the surface of the water is evidence of some degree of pollution. Never allow the water to reach the stage you often see in dykes and ditches of becoming a smoky blueish colour. If it does the oxygen content is likely to be very low indeed and a very thorough cleaning-up operation is needed. But your pond should never reach that stage. An occasional clearing of dead leaves during the summer, a thinning of oxygenators from time to time, and a cutting back of dead

foliage in autumn is really all that is required to keep the pond healthy — a self-perpetuating eco-system. Some owners of concrete ponds lower the water level from time to time to scrub the walls clean of algae — liners can be washed and rubbed down too — but I would only carry out this operation very occasionally, if at all. A certain amount of algae is always present. It can best be kept in check by underwater plants; but if blanket weed forms this should be removed by hand or twirled out on the end of a stick.

Fish ailments and pests

Fish are susceptible to quite a few ailments and pests; but one pest constitutes a greater threat than all others combined. And sadly, I know of no satisfactory remedy. That pest is the heron. Should you happen to live anywhere near a river or heronry, then sooner or later your pond is likely to be visited by one of these birds. Even a small sheet of water is very conspicuous from the sky and a heron in the vicinity can hardly fail to notice it. They are shy birds, easily frightened by the appearance of human beings. But what they lack in courage they certainly make up for in perseverance. At odd, quiet hours, especially around dawn, a heron will not hesitate to land in a built-up area if he knows there is food for the taking. Goldfish are easy prey and a heron can devastate, indeed wipe out, one's entire stock of fish. If he does not do so on one visit, be assured he will return so long as there are more fish to be caught. In my experience, the most likely time for this unwelcome visitor to arrive is in winter when food may be scarce, especially after heavy rain when the local river is in a muddied spate.

In many countries, herons are protected by law. And rightly so, for they are graceful, lovely creatures in flight, and their tranquil, placid silhouette on many a river bank or estuary — if not in the garden — is surely a

Pitfalls, problems and pond care

RIGHT *This picture is not upside down. The Water Boatman, Noto-necta glauca, is suspended from the water surface.*

LEFT *The Great Diving Beetle, Dystiscus marginalis; a greedy, carnivorous creature with a life span of several years. They are about 30–35 mm. long in the adult stage, and the larvae, which are even bigger, are also predatory.*

sight worth preserving. You could remove your fish to an indoor aquarium to protect them from this danger during the winter months. But this may not be feasible if you have a large stock of fish, and besides, it does not protect the fish from a possible visit in summer. A small pond can be netted over in winter, but again the heron may arrive when the net is off; and if you are growing plants around the margin of the pool, then you have the added irritation of the plants growing through the net in early spring before you may feel it is safe to remove it. And bear in mind too that a heron has no compunction about sticking his long beak through netting with even small holes. I have known the birds both to walk on plastic netting and raise it up at one corner. So the netting should be firmly secured at the water's edge and raised above the pond by placing a pole or similar object in the centre of it. The only foolproof method of keeping herons away is not often practicable. If your pond is enclosed by walls or rustic poles (with very narrow gaps between vertical and horizontal poles), then you may be able to stretch plastic netting over the whole enclosure. The poles or walls must be situated so as not to interfere with the amount of sunlight the pond receives.

Cats take a malicious pleasure in standing by the pool's edge and whipping fish out. Friendly fish who come up to the surface on the sight of a human being may well do the same for a cat. A well-aimed missile will put off most cats from repeating the experiment.

There are a number of insects which may attack small fish and fry. The Great Diving Beetle, *Dystiscus marginalis*, and others of the genus, are carnivorous and will feed off fish, snails, tadpoles and insects. They fly from pond to pond so they cannot be entirely excluded. The Water Boatman, the most common of the species being *Notonecta glauca,* has a powerful pair of stylets with which it can make short work of tadpoles and small fish. The Water Scorpion,*Nepa cinerea,* takes hold of its victim with a strong pair of front legs and then sucks the blood of its captive like a vampire. The larva of the dragonfly possesses a so-called mask, a kind of jaw with powerful hooks.

A dragonfly larva revealing its ferocious face mask.

129

These are used to snatch and grip passing prey, fish being among the victims.

To prey and be preyed upon is part of the unalterable cycle of the pond, indeed it is of the essence of all natural life. To break the cycle is well nigh impossible. Hand picking or removing by net a number of these creatures is possible — in particular the Diving Beetle — but their eradication is not. From the many eggs that mature goldfish may lay and which hatch out, only a tiny proportion reach adulthood. Only the most stringently controlled conditions can raise the survival rate significantly. The pond owner must, I think, be satisfied with the way of nature in what is a relatively natural environment. Adult fish can be expected to contain the population of these enemies. And although enemies to fish, the activity of the Water Boatman and the Water Scorpion as they scurry about the pond, as well as many other insects, is surely an intrinsic element of interest in any water garden.

Remedial action should, however, be taken in the case of an infestation of Anchor worms or fish lice. The Anchor worms attach themselves to the skin of the fish and there is usually a slight swelling at the point of entry. They can grow up to almost 2 cm. Fish lice are very much smaller, 5-6 mm., and when they attach themselves to a fish, it is common to see the fish dashing wildly around the pond for no apparent reason. In both cases remove the affected fish and, holding it firmly in a wet cloth — but without squeezing it unduly — take out the parasite with a pair of tweezers. Treat the point of entry with iodine or a little household disinfectant; or paint the parasite with paraffin oil which will kill it. Examine the rest of your fish stock and treat in the same way as necessary.

These parasites may be introduced with plants taken from the wild. Before placing in your pond, new plants can be disinfected with potassium permanganate. A few grains of the chemical in a bucket of water in which the plants can be submerged will serve the purpose. A complete pond can also be disinfected, and potassium permanganate will also cut down the algae growth and improve the clarity of the water. The danger is, of course, that the fish will be poisoned by the chemical, fry in particular, and so far as clear water is concerned the measure can only be regarded as temporary. So I would use it only as a last resort. Make up a saturated solution of the chemical and introduce it to the pond at the rate of two teaspoonfuls for every ten litres of water.

White Spot is the common name of another parasite made evident by the rash of white dots that may run over the skins and fins of the fish. It should not be confused with the little dots that may appear on the gill plates of cock fish during the mating season. It is more common in tropical tanks than outdoor pools. The White Spot parasite is dependent upon hosts, so that if you can remove your livestock from the pool, hopefully the parasite will be eradicated. The affected fish are best placed in running water for a week or more, if you can rig up an aquarium under a tap. Alternatively, add ten to fifteen drops of $2\frac{1}{2}$ per cent solution of mercurochrome to every ten litres of still water.

A salt bath is the answer if you find your fish suffering from leeches, easily recognized by their worm-like appearance with a disc at either end, and by their length: up to 2.5 cm. Begin with four teaspoonfuls of salt (sea salt is best if obtainable) dissolved in every ten litres of water, and increase the amount of salt daily unless the fish shows signs of distress. This is also the stock treatment for the more serious problem of fungus (although your aquarist can supply a fancy range of chemicals for this, as for many fish ailments. Some chemicals, however, may tend to make your fish infertile). The fungus *Saprolegnia ferox* is normally present in water, but fish are unlikely to become infected with it unless they are wounded in some way or are in a poor state of health. Overfed fish are less resistant to infection than those properly fed. The infection is visible as greyish-white strands, or as if cotton wool was adhering to the fish. As well as the salt bath, which should be changed daily, the affected area on the fish can be painted with diluted iodine.

Constipation should not be a problem with outdoor fish which have a varied diet. When it occurs the symptoms are sluggishness and the excrement is lengthy and knotted. Hard and dry foodstuffs and overfeeding are often the cause. Fish may right themselves, but you can transfer them for twenty-four hours to a tank containing Epsom salts at the rate of six tablespoonfuls to every six litres of water. Dried foods should be avoided for a while and chopped earthworms substituted.

For dropsy, evident by the manner in which the scales of the fish stand out and the general puffy appearance of the fish, there is no known cure. Similarly, fish whose sense of balance has been affected are usually best destroyed. One can try placing the fish in a tank heated to about 20-22°C., feeding it on earthworms and trying Epsom salts, but the results are rarely successful. Despite the long list of ailments and parasites to which fish can fall victim, one can expect few casualties among fish that are not overfed and which live in a well-oxygenated pond.

A problem of which I have been the unwitting cause is worth mentioning, for many pond owners must be in the same position. No text book of which I know warns against it. That is the danger of removing fish, and not only small ones, when removing clumps of overgrown weed. If you grow *Elodea,* for example, fish can easily lurk unseen in this weed and when a large number of strands are drawn up in a bunch, a fish trapped in the middle is quite powerless to make his presence known. Having transferred sizeable clumps of weed to tanks I have, on occasion, been surprised to find a fish or two swimming round in the tank a few days later. Their fate would have been quite different had the weed been intended for the rubbish dump. So do examine your surplus weed with care.

Finally, let me end this chapter by mentioning the greatest pitfall of all in owning a pond, the problem I mentioned in the first page of the book. Any depth of water is a hazard to children. Nothing attracts the young in a garden more than a pond. And nothing in a garden are they more likely to enjoy. But toddlers are only compatible with ponds if under supervision.

GARDEN

Memories telescope the years for all of us. So they do for me at this moment. In my mind's eye I can see quite clearly a student alternately looking at his books strewn across a table, and gazing out of the window on to a bare stretch of lawn. The room is cast in shadow and to me, the student, tired of my books, it seems dank and tiresome. Outside the autumn sun warms a crisp morning in September. It is a morning to be out and about; and the desire to be out and about is never stronger than when one has to be inside, spending long hours in studious silence. At such a time the mind grows vacant, and in being vacant, susceptible to unsought ideas.

And it was then, quite suddenly, that the idea of building a pond sprang upon me. Perhaps the bareness of the lawn or my restiveness was the cause. I cannot tell. But the vision of a pond, stocked with agile fish, well planted with colourful aquatics and marginal plants, was there before me with an irresistible clarity. The garden, it was obvious, would be transformed. But little could I have guessed the extent to which the pond would affect me, becoming, in fact, close on a daily preoccupation. Entries taken from an old diary tell the tale:

January 6 Rose as usual at 7.15 a.m. and pulled back the curtains to gaze at the pond. That has been my habit for two years or more, since the pond was built. And I do not believe it has ever looked exactly the same twice, not only because I have been constantly adding plants and hopefully making improvements, but also because nature never really pauses, even in winter. Growth, decay and change are always present. These mornings darkness obscures all but the outline of the rockery around the pond, the pond's edge and the sheet of water, and the silhouette of one or two of the taller marginals. The *Typha* dominate the scene, still tall and stately despite the ravages of winter. I have *Typha latifolia* planted in a pocket on the left-hand side and *Typha angustifolia* in a sort of shallow bay on the right. Unless it is lashing rain, after breakfast, I cross the lawn and the little bridge over the pond to enter the garage. I could, if I wished, go out the front door and reach the garage along the pavement. But that would mean I could not pause at the pond's edge. This morning there is a heavy dew and I begin the day with wet shoes. Myriads of dewdrops cling to what remains of the Sweet Galingale, most of which — too much — was cut for indoor decoration last autumn, and there are drops too on what remains of the sad, drooping leaves of the Marsh Marigold. But they will soon pick up in the coming months. A spider who has spun his web in the cleft of a Japanese Maple on the rockery has received overnight a thousand dewdrops. I wonder if he finds the result as spectacularly beautiful as we do. Probably not, all that extra weight and moisture may be to him a great nuisance. And what fly or insect would be so silly as to fly headlong into something so conspicuous?

January 9 Watching the sun just touch the edge at one side of the pond this morning, a thought suddenly occurred to me. The pond is divided into two large halves, one quite deep and the other shallow, and joined by a narrow channel over which runs the bridge.

It is the shallow half that receives the sun first and loses it last. Had I designed the pond so that the deeper half received the sun first and last, it would warm up more quickly and the deep water-lilies would flower just that little bit earlier. If we were to do everything twice how perfect the world might be.

January 24 The advance of the month and the fact that I rose a little later than usual, meant that the rising sun had quite covered half of the pond before I pulled my curtains. I hastened out to the bridge before breakfast. The air was sharp and utterly still, the sky lightly ribbed with white and red-streaked clouds. The water provided a perfect mirror image, broken only by one of the rubber balls which had stuck fast to a leaf of Water Hawthorn. A single goldfish, one of the larger ones, cruises slowly round in the deepest part. He is presumably looking for food, but is in no great need of it. The rest of the fish that I have left outdoors are either completely hidden in the dense foliage of *Elodea* or are but partly visible. I can pick out the odd streak of gold here and there, the back or tail of a goldfish or Shubunkin. A morning like this, the clearness and stillness makes one expectant of spring, but the weather is unlikely to remain so calm for long. I dally at the pond's edge visualizing the growth to come and return indoors to hard toast and lukewarm coffee.

January 27 The weather forecast on the radio this morning blithely declared that snow could be expected in the north of the country. That was reason enough to expect snow here in the south. Sure enough by evening the first of the snow arrived. I stood on the bridge watching the flakes fall soundlessly into the water, disappearing into the depths for ever. On the rockery a few flakes perched temporarily on the heather and junipers, but only on the rocks did the snow remain. In the fading light the pond looked gaunt and old.

January 28 It has snowed during the night and the whole garden is blanketed. What a contrast to last night when the rockery looked so patchy. The pond, however, has not frozen and looks like an ugly black gash in the pure white landscape. I do not want to spoil this pristine sight by marking the snow with footprints, but Cliff (our young Jack Russell terrier) is soon haring round the garden, sending up great flurries of snow in his wake. I watch his joy for several minutes until he turns to the rockery. The thought of crocuses making their way up only to be churned out of the ground makes me roar at him. He returns to the house very crest-fallen.

February 1 The temperature has dropped several degrees over the last few days and more snow has fallen. The junipers, especially *Juniperus sabina* 'Blue Danube' with its overlapping branches pointing slightly upwards, spread out with their white coverings and occasional markings of dark green, look extraordinarily impressive. I gingerly try walking on the pond and to my delight find that it bears my weight. There is no need to keep a hole open for the fish. I am confident that the depth of the pool and the fact that there is very little decaying matter on the bottom means the oxygen level of the water will remain high and the toxic gases low. Beneath the ice I can make out the shapes of fish quite clearly. The Golden Orfe, in particular, seem to be on the move. Is it the vibration of my footsteps that has them agitated? As I move about they scurry away to left and right. When I tread more softly they remain still longer, but are still reluctant to allow me to pass right over them. A slight tapping of my heel makes them dart about in agitation. Fish are highly sensitive to vibration.

February 3 The temperature has risen again. I find out the hard way. Took a whim to skate over the ice on the way to the garage this morning. The ice cracked at the shallow end which gets the early sun. Returned to the house to change socks, shoes and trousers. In the afternoon, Peter came in from next door on some pretext and headed straight for the pond. I warned him to no avail. The ice held for him at the deep end. I then, maliciously, threw some coins near the spot where I went in. To my secret disappointment, that bore his light weight and he went off with a handsome profit.

February 7 The snow has turned to slush and the garden looks miserable. The plants on the rockery are sodden and downcast. The innumerable small stones and pebbles seem to have emerged from the muddy soil giving the rockery an unpleasant gravelly appearance. I suppose this is caused by the soil sinking with the weight of melting ice and snow. Once the soil has dried out sufficiently I will rake it well over.

February 26 What stamina crocuses possess. They were out today in the midst of radiant sunshine, and it must be a month or more since they first appeared. (Pity that the leaves give the rockery a slightly tatty appearance once the flowers are finally over.) But they make a pretty, welcoming appearance at this time of year in conjunction with Winter Aconite, *Chinodoxa, Scilla, Gallanthus* and the two early heathers I have planted, *Erica* 'Springwood White' and *carnea*. Planted in dense clumps these little bulbs do much to remove the bleakness of the pond during the winter months. I notice that a few of the crocuses have had trouble showing above the branches of the prostrate junipers and heathers. This is indicative of how rapidly these evergreen plants can grow in a few seasons.

When planting the bulbs I put them in well clear of the junipers' spreading branches.

March 7 Spring has now truly arrived at the pond. For the last few days *Rhododendron praecox* with their delicate but rich shade of violet flowers have been in full bloom. Bulbs, even when flowering in quantity, do no more than contribute colouring to their surroundings. These rhododendrons are really magnificent plants; though not much more than a metre high, any of them, they all dominate their surroundings. The whole area around the pond seems to be filled with colour while the *praecox* lasts. They begin a firmer shade of violet than they end. In the sunshine the trumpet flowers appear quite pale and light. But when viewed in the fading light of a March afternoon, their colour becomes altogether richer, the flowers almost seeming to emit their own light. While everything else around the pond (bulbs apart) begins to disappear into the dusk, the rhododendrons remain conspicuous and brilliant right into the end of the day. I can think of few pleasures to equal standing by the pool in the half light of a March evening admiring these gorgeous plants, hearing an occasional gurgle as a goldfish rises to the surface, seeing the purplish ripples gently cross the pool and stop; and then become aware of utter silence returning again. Fed the fish for the first time this year, just a few flakes. Felt cold after being by the pool for some time, so returned to the house to curl up by the fire with a book and a glass of port.

March 22 Hard frost and bitter East winds have alternated with each other over the past weeks. The rhododendrons are now on the wane. Indeed of the seven plants I possess, three have now lost their blooms entirely. They are, without exception, those situated where the morning sun reaches them before the frost has melted off their blooms. This shortens the life of the blooms to a marked degree. Having been out of the house all day, I looked forward to spending a few minutes by the pond before supper. But the wind swung into the West during the afternoon to bring rain. As I write this now it is simply lashing out of the heavens as the radio forecast warned at breakfast time. I did not believe a word of it.

March 23 Having read late into the night, I woke up more sleepily than usual and stared sightlessly out on the damp morning. Then a sight half-hidden by a boulder woke me up with a start. I could just make out the grey, thin form of a heron. So well did his colour merge with the surrounding soil and rockery that I doubt if I should have noticed him but for the slight jerk he made as I pulled back the curtains. I immediately banged the window. He cocked his head to one side, and then flew off on those great ponderous wings. I dressed as quickly as possible and rushed down to the pond to count the fish. The weed is too dense to be absolutely certain of counting them all. I poked round with a long stick. It is amazing how well the fish recognize danger. Normally, if I were to run a stick or net through the weeds, the fish would simply swim off to a quieter spot; but now they try to bury themselves into the bottom of the pond as far out of sight as possible. I counted only eight Golden Orfe and there should be fifteen. Two goldfish and one Shubunkin appear to be missing too. I do not know why the Golden Orfe should suffer the largest number of casualties. Just as I was returning to the house in disgust I spotted a goldfish half over on its side nearly hidden by a rock near the bottom of the waterfall. Closer inspection revealed that it had a nasty wound along one flank and a cut across the back. The heron was probably about to gorge the fish when I disturbed him and dropped it in his haste. Of course it happens to be the tamest of all my goldfish.

136

All last summer I fed him on worms and morsels direct from my fingers. He was, I suppose, the most vulnerable by being the least shy. I blame myself for not covering the pond. Netting the fish as gently as I could, I brought him indoors to a mild salt bath. I would not be optimistic about his chances, however. I had breakfast by the window, and not quarter of an hour after I had frightened the heron off, I saw him return and circle round before I ran into the garden. Doubtless the heavy rain last night has coloured the local rivers and food is scarce. I am determined to build an arched wall right round the pond and stretch a net overhead. It is the only answer.

March 27 The daffodils are out in all their colourfulness now, but I made a mistake in planting them on the rockery at all. They are too tall and out of proportion to the rest of the plants. A few miniature narcissi would look much happier situated beside the little maples and under the willow. When the trees have grown larger there will be time enough for the larger daffodils. John B., an enthusiastic gardener, came over in the late afternoon. He asked me if I had both the single and double forms of Marsh Marigold. I pointed out the two plants, remarking that I expected the single to flower first. No, he countered, the double always comes out first. I distinctly remembered the single coming out first last year and told him so. But he remained adamant, so it remains to be seen. The sick fish has not developed fungus infection in his wound, but he looks very low in the aquarium where I have placed him, lying on the bottom breathing heavily and with effort.

April 2 I am right. Two flowers of the single Marsh Marigold opened today, later than last year but still ahead of the double variety. I rang John in glee. He is nonplussed and simply replied that none of his is out yet.

Crossing the bridge this morning I did a 'double take' in suddenly noticing that the lilies have moved, a number of red leaf shoots were quite apparent. The recent mild spell has evidently warmed up the pool and stirred the lilies into life. The sick fish showed very little sign of life or movement in the aquarium before I left the house. He had keeled over slightly to one side. This evening, on my return, he was on the surface, dead.

April 7 The frogs have left their hidey-holes in force over the last few days and are now happily mating in the pond. There must be thirty or more pairs. How such small bodies can produce such a mass of spawn is difficult to understand. It is spread over more than a metre. My mind goes back to the school pond. At morning break, as schoolboys, we would rush to the pond's edge in spring to watch scores of frogs frantically joined in copulation. If a master appeared we would back away from the pond, sheepishly. I doubt if today's school children would be so coy. I have heard it said that a bullfrog, in his enthusiasm, is capable of mounting a fish by mistake and strangling it to death. I very much doubt if that is possible and certainly have never seen it happen. The frogs invariably lay their spawn in the shallowest part of the pond, presumably because it is warmer. Difference of temperature may also explain why frogs emerge to mate at widely different times even in a comparatively small locality. The same reason could hardly explain why John's double Marsh Marigold came out before his single, whereas the opposite was true for me. He rang me triumphantly this evening. 'We're quits,' he announced.

April 11 Simon R. bought me round a small tuber of *Nymphaea* 'Laydekeri Purpurata', which he had promised me last year. I thanked him profusely and mumbled something about hoping he had not lifted it too early in the year. There is still comparatively little growth in the pond. The Water Hawthorn has reached the surface but none of the water-lilies has, and the water is still chilly. I wished Simon had waited another fortnight or more when all the plants would be on the move. I visited David yesterday to admire his *Orontium*. What a fine specimen it is. He has it planted in more than half a metre of water, nearer three-quarters I would say, and the leaves float on the surface while the white and yellow flowers emerge from the water quite erect. I have been promised a piece later.

April 21 I had the luck to have to take the three-hour train journey from Dublin to Cork today, I got to the station early to be certain of a window seat. As I had anticipated, all along the canals, along practically every river and rivulet, pond and lake, there was an abundance of Marsh Marigold. The strength of that yellow is nothing if not extraordinary. Wherever the plant is to be found it radiates a brilliant warmth, be it in ditch, on river bank or moist meadow. While the rest of the carriage carried on an inane conversation about some football controversy, I happily whiled away the hours with my nose pressed up against the window pane like a child. Of the several hundred passengers aboard, I do not suppose more than half a dozen actually took the trouble to notice these lovely plants or the Bog Bean (though far less obvious at a distance). And I daresay many a confirmed gardener might pass them by too, and for no other reason than the plants are neither rare nor come from foreign shores. No man is a prophet ... as they say, and no plant either. I returned home about seven, by which time the light breeze had cooled and taken on that unmistakable tang of new growth. It was sheer ecstasy. As the sun sank I pondered over the day's work seated on a rock by the pond, breathing in the air and admiring still the humble Marsh Marigold. Actually, its

other name, King Cup, describes it more appropriately. Like the *praecox*, the dimming light seems only to heighten its brilliance.

April 27 The two or three sprigs of Bog Bean that I collected two years ago have filled one corner of the pond, and the superb little flowers are now at their peak of beauty. The Bog Bean is abundant throughout the wetlands and it is strange to think that a thousand cows must daily have the privilege of crushing into the mud one of the most exquisite of all water-loving plants. Happily, the Bog Bean can well take such treatment.

April 29 The recent spell of sunny weather has given the water a slight cloudy tinge. It will only be temporary. The tips of the *elodeas* are now a vivid light green — a sign of growth — and they will clear the pond in no time.

May 4 As if by magic the water was crystal clear this morning, whereas only yesterday it was less than perfect. I examined Simon's lily 'Laydekeri Purpurata': it had sent up no shoots and on lifting it I discovered the tuber had begun to rot. I know what I should have done: placed it in the greenhouse in a shallow bowl. The magpies may not have helped. Having put the lily basket in shallow water, the birds paddled in the mud probably with a view to catching tadpoles which are wriggling round in their thousands, but also damaging any young shoots that may possibly have appeared. I spotted a Common Newt seemingly nibbling at a piece of *Potamogeton crispus*. He saw me too and fled into a clump of *Myriophyllum*. I presume there must be more newts about and that they have entered the pond to mate. But I have seen only one batch of their eggs, laid out like a string of pearls.

May 7 Finding that the writing was going badly, I sauntered down to the pond for a short break. Predictably the short break turned into something longer. I became engrossed in watching a small hatch of Mayfly *(Emphemera danica)* brought on by the recent warm weather. The nymphs were rising, struggling to the surface, anxiously kicking and fighting their way out of their penultimate coats to become duns; then flying, none too skilfully, to trees, bushes and marginals (where I lost sight of them) to moult again and become, if only for a day, graceful hovering spinners. Quite why these insects should be called Mayfly is something of a mystery. The largest hatches nearly always take place in June and sometimes there are none at all in May. Could it have anything to do with the change of the calendar?

May 10   The pond is now, for the first time this year, a mass of colour. Aubretia and phlox in purple, red and white, colour the rockery. In the bog garden the little *Calla palustris* or Bog Arum is fully out as are the *Lysichitum americanun* plants in the opposite corner. *Ranunculus aconitifolius,* the White Bachelor's Buttons, is blossoming (it needs to be cleared of weeds that have sprung up around it), and the *Primula pulverulenta* are about to burst forth. The Marsh Marigold is far from over, the double is just about at its height, and behind all, though creeping forward somewhat, is the lovely *Polygonum bistort.* In the pond itself, the Water Crowfoot is producing its little white flowers, the small leaves of the *Villarsia* 'Bennettii' or Water Fringe are beginning to dot the surface and the Water Hawthorn has several blossoms fully open. And the Water Gladiole, Tongue Buttercup and the reeds are all shooting skywards.

May 15   The electrician came to repair the electric cable to the pond. It was a new man and I brought him down the garden to show him where the cable was laid. He stood looking around at the pond and the rockery for a few moments and then said: 'Where did you get all those rocks from?' That is always the first question anyone who has no interest in gardening asks. The second is where did you buy all those fish? Sure enough our new electrician asked me that too.

May 17   We had invited a few friends in for drinks and got a superb morning for it. Sitting, walking and talking around the pond we whiled away a few hours in as pleasant a way as I think possible. All I missed was the tinkling of the waterfall which I have yet to connect to the new cable.

May 20   I went round to David to obtain a root of his Golden Club which he promised to divide. He put on a hefty pair of waders and entered the pond, actually it is more like a lake. After ten minutes he had become truly stuck in the mud without having had any success in dividing the plant. I gave him the handle of a rake to extricate him, and after much pulling and heaving he managed to get back to the shore. The roots of *Orontium aquaticum* are very tenacious. Needless to say I went home without the plant.

May 29   Since we use a great deal of water mint with our potatoes I decided to add to our stock of plants, which before summer's end are usually denuded of leaves. I strolled down the bank of the local stream, through the meadow and on through two more fields as far as the swamp and I found only one meagre plant at the very end. I could have sworn all along the bank there were clumps of the plant last year. On the return journey, I walked through the fields at a distance of about five or six metres from the stream. I suddenly came across an abundance of water mint partially concealed in the long grass. It is curious that it should not be growing at the water's edge but in the drier - though still moist - soil some distance away. It only goes to show how often a plant will thrive in one particular place - not always the most obvious one - and make no headway a few metres to left or right.

June 4 All the water-lilies now have several flower buds each. The earliest to actually flower was 'Marliacea Chromatella' which opened briefly just before midday yesterday. The wind turned to the East immediately after lunch and the bloom closed again like a clam. One would expect *Nymphaea alba* to be the first to bloom since it is the native lily, used to our moderate temperatures, but it will be several days yet before its first bud even breaks the surface. 'James Brydon' is likely to be the last to bloom as the buds are still close to the crown. But this lily is well worth waiting for, not only on account of the beauty of the flower, but also because it throws up so many in proportion to the number of leaves.

June 6 The first flower of 'Chromatella' has now sunk back. How short a time they last, but it has beem replaced by two further blooms. 'Escarboucle' has one small bloom out too. It is slightly tinged with white, so I presume it comes from a young tuber off the mainstock. I must say the blotched appearance of young 'Escarboucle' blooms look almost like a disease, they remind me of alopecia. However, one has no choice but to wait for the plant to mature. John was on the phone to enquire if any of my lilies were out. I said my first came out four days ago. He immediately retorted that all his plants had been in flower a fortnight ago. I know how he does it. He lays a sheet of polythene over the pond in early spring. It has the same effect as a glass-house. I should dislike the sight of polythene straddling the pond while the rockery is so colourful and should you get a late frost after removing the polythene, all that accelerated growth would have been for nothing.

June 19 Every time I cross the bridge and look to left and right, I am irritated by the fact that the water level in the right-hand part appears lower than in the left. The reason is, of course, that proper account was not taken of the level of the ground when the pond was dug out. The difference is very slight but still annoying. However, the Brooklime has all but concealed the bare concrete. It is a vigorous plant and I like the shiny, wax-like green leaves, but the tiny blue flowers are too small to provide much colour. I might think of substituting something else.

June 26 If I were to choose one day out of the year as showing the pond in its absolute prime, then this would be the one. I counted twenty-one lilies in full bloom this morning: four *alba*; four 'Froebeli'; three 'James Brydon'; five 'Chromatella'; three 'Escarboucle' (all pure red) and two 'Moorei'. The irises are resplendent too. *Iris pseudacorus* still has a few blooms and a few buds left; *laevigata* is just about at its height and *sibirica* is flowering more profusely than even last year. I have the Irises grouped round the pond in pockets about one and a half metres long at a stretch. This spreads the colour over the whole area. The Tongue Buttercup is now in flower too and will provide colour from now until early autumn. And the variegated foliage of *Acorus*, *Scirpus tabernaemontani zebrinus* and *Glyceria* will make a striking display until the end of summer and indeed well into the autumn.

June 28 It is amusing how a plant will surreptitiously move itself from a position it does not like to a more congenial one. I put in a few young shoots of *Myosotis* in the damp soil close to the *Typha angustifolia*. Now after a few seasons it has spread round behind the *Typha*, presumably to avail of the cool, moist shade the tall leaves of the bulrush provide.

140

June 29 This was an afternoon to which I had been looking forward: afternoon tea at Rosemary's. And it could not have turned out more perfectly, for it was a sultry, cloudless day with not a breeze to disturb as much as a leaf. We walked the garden up and down, examining each plant in turn. Far away could be heard the occasional hum of a car, a sound made tiny in comparison with the chuckling sparrows at the pond's edge, the crows calling lazily overhead and the busy passing sounds of many insects. In this spacious, old world garden, full of gravelled paths, sweet-smelling herbs, foxgloves, irises, poppies and columbine, lupins, climbing roses, hydrangeas, honeysuckle and buddleias, one could as well be in the depths of the country as in a town. And what could be a more congenial setting for sipping afternoon tea? We sat, as always, by the pond, and discussed a thousand questions on lilies and marginals, which plants to thin back, which plants to divide and share. The sun was glinting through the poplars as I walked home, full of hot buttered scones, chocolate cake — and a warm feeling of wellbeing.

June 3 The little red flowers of Water Milfoil look very effective against the white of the Crowfoot and the occasional flower of *Elodea densa;* but perhaps too much of the surface area is covered, indeed cluttered with plants. The water-lilies have spread out a good deal and are vying for space not only with the Crowfoot and Water Hawthorn, but *Villarsia,* a very vigorous grower, and the Water Soldier which has come up to the surface in abundance. Greet, the Dutch au pair from next door, was in this evening and looking aghast said: 'You don't grow that, do you?' pointing at the *Stratiotes.* I nodded: 'Why not?' She explained that in Holland it is so prolific that it clutters up many ditches and small waterways. I said it was a rarity in this part of the world and was, in any case,

a most attractive plant. She wrinkled her nose sceptically and laughed. The broad, matt colours of the *Iris kaempferi* were what appealed to her. 'They are ten a penny on the rice paddies of Japan,' I remarked. She laughed again.

July 5 I spent a pleasant afternoon wading through the pond thinning out *Elodea canadensis* which had become very bushy indeed. I do not like stirring up the pond during the height of summer but if I leave it until autumn it means removing essential winter cover. I am amazed at how unfearful the fish are at my presence. They come right up to where I am pulling out the weed, curious to see what is going on. How utterly different is their behaviour when a heron is about. How do they distinguish friend from foe? They must have some means of relaying danger one to the other, but I am not aware of any research into this. Out of interest, I placed a few handfuls of *Elodea* in the empty aquarium along with a few scoopings of mud, just to see what insect life they contain. The pond was quite coloured by the time I had finished the job, but by leaving the waterfall running it had begun to clear perceptibly within four or five hours and will be back to its usual state in a matter of days.

July 7 I examined the aquarium since it had cleared and discovered quite a variety of life. I found: a Water Scorpion, a Great Diving Beetle (pretty sick I would think, not much movement out of him), a Water Boatman and a dead Pond Skater. There were numerous shrimps and a Caddis Fly larva, I think *Limnephilus flavicornis,* which seemed to be attempting to add to its cumbersome shell by playing around with a tiny stone. There were also a number of blood worms, *Tubifex,* waving their thin, bright red bodies around for all they were worth and I glimpsed a leech, wriggling its way through the water at speed.

141

July 12 Time loses its meaning in July. One can just lie at the pond's edge watching the great rolling clouds drift into and out of the water, follow the Golden Orfe and goldfish and Shubunkins on their endless travels through the weeds; and gaze thoughtlessly at the lily blooms, the bright colours of the Monkey Flower, red, yellow and orange; and one can listen to the whispering of the wind through Reed Mace, Bulrush and Galingale. On such a day as today, the worries of the world recede and lose their meaning.

July 16 We have been exceptionally lucky with the weather this month. I cannot remember for how many consecutive days now we have had supper at the edge of the pool. And once the table is put out the fish immediately swim over to share whatever titbits we throw in. Since we usually have a salad, there is hard-boiled egg, well chopped, to spare.

July 23 While visiting a nearby public garden this afternoon, I noticed they had obtained a fine mass of *Cotula coronopifolia*, Brass Buttons. I immediately thought of where this low growing, dense plant could fit into the scheme of my own pond. I approached a gardener and to my joy found that he could not identify the plant. Would he mind if I took a small piece away to have it identified? Not at all, so with his imprimatur I was able to march past the official at the gate with impunity. It was a neat variation on the 'tie your shoe lace' subterfuge. Where the *Veronica beccabunga* currently conceals the cement edge I shall plant the *Cotula*; it is more colourful.

July 26 Today I noticed more honey bees than usual crawling around the edge of the pond or alighting on lily leaves. This is a sure sign that the honey flow in the area is over.

The nectar bees collect from flowers contains a high percentage of moisture. When nectar is scarce, the bees supplement their water supply by visiting the pond.

July 27 Despite the high winds, I visited Mount Usher in Ashford this morning. I need not have worried. The winds, so far from detracting from the ferns, added to them. I walked through the fernery and I experienced something quite different from their usual tranquility in watching their fronds flash dramatically forward and backwards. My favourite display of Astilbes are to be found at Mount Usher. There the plants are grouped all around the bog gardens, around which one can walk on numerous paths. The shrubs and trees conceal one area from another; and every new area that you enter has its own set of surprises, its own style.

August 1 The last month of summer, and the most opulent one. But even in the midst of opulence there are signs of decay. All the water-lilies have yellow and frayed leaves. I have tried to cut them off and remove them, also some of the green leaves, so that the ratio of leaves to flowers is improved. The Japanese Arrowhead is about to flower and so is the *Alisma* and Bog Cotton. *Sagittaria* always seems to fascinate children. Padraig and Niamh were in before supper. Padraig fingered the top of an Arrowhead leaf to see if it was sharp. Then he asked why it was standing in water. 'So it can drink,' I replied; 'We all have to do that to survive.' 'But what about the plants that are not in the water?' he queried. I could see I was in for a question-and-answer session. 'They are able to take water from the soil too, it is just that on the bank there is less moisture.' He paused for a moment and I thought his mind had moved elsewhere. Then he asked, 'How do they drink water?' I picked an Arrowhead leaf, held it up to the light and pointed out the veins. 'There,' I said, 'the leaf uses all those veins just the way you use a drinking straw.' I have rarely seen such a sense of wonder enter a child's eyes. 'All leaves are a bit like that,' I added, and he marched off round the garden picking leaves and holding them up to the light.

August 10 The sense of balance that I had achieved by planting *Typha angustifolia* at one end of the pond and *latifolia* at the other has come undone, since *latifolia* has left its neat pocket and taken large strides across the pond. Once the pokers have matured in September when they can be cut for indoor decoration, I intend cutting out the plant entirely and replacing it with *Typha minima*. That will restore the balance permanently.

August 18 Gazing into the pool near the bridge I suddenly spotted a fish no more than a centimetre long. I had never seen it before, and closer inspection of the water revealed a number of minute fish, no thicker than the stem of a pin. Presumably, they have hatched quite recently.

August 26 Returned from a weekend in Paris at 3. a.m., having had to land at Cork and take a train up. I should have been home at 4 p.m. yesterday, but heavy fog over the whole country delayed departure by some ten hours. The tedious wait was more than worthwhile. I shall not easily forget the sight of the pond through that heavy morning mist. The bulrushes looked weird with their pokers emerging at intervals through the vague light. The prostrate junipers stretched out unmoving branches, dripping at the water's edge. Their character seemed quite changed by the fog, eerie, and yet splendid in a strange way. From the water, the *Alisma* flower stems rose like new-fangled aerials, and the lily pads seemed to be floating on nothing, or like clouds suspended in time and air. There

was no sound, except an occasional dripping of water off leaves, or the plop of a frog disappearing into the pond for safety. The garden was full of them, I counted fifteen before giving up, picking my way gingerly between them, across the bridge, over the lawn and so to bed.

September 3 What stamina the *Mimulus, Myosotis* and *Veronica beccabunga* possess. This will be their third month in flower. True, the *beccabunga* is almost over and the Myosotis is throwing up fewer blooms, but I expect the *Mimulus* to continue to flower until the first frosts, maybe even a little after. The *Pontederia* is in full bloom.

September 10 There is an autumn stillness over the pond now, almost a hushed quietness. The earth is beginning to smell raw again with heavy dews. The pokers of the bulrushes have turned a rich brown and the Water Fringe is flowering yet; the Pickerel Weed, *Mimulus* and the foliage of the Manna Grass, which is obtaining its autumn tint along with the maples, are the main centres of attraction, with the water-lilies of course. We savour the last few days reminiscent of summer warmth, having morning coffee by the pool when at home. The fish have become less agile; with the dropping of the temperature they move more slowly and spend longer amongst the weeds.

September 25 Faithful to the last, 'Froebeli' is still flowering profusely. There were three blooms this afternoon. 'Chromatella' produced one as did 'Escarboucle' yesterday. It is interesting to note how much longer the blooms remain open in autumn, right up till late afternoon. In summer the flowers are much more sensitive to changes in temperature. This is especially true if the temperature is exceptionally high in the morning. Once it drops in the afternoon, be it only a few

143

degrees, the flowers quickly close up. Now, in late September, the flowers remain open for hours, impervious to the chilling wind.

October 3 The first frosts are upon us. The season of the pond is now over. I have little to do but clear away the dead leaves and snip off most of those still green. There is hardly any point in leaving them now. The next fine day I shall cut back the leaves of the marginals. It is slightly sad to see the end of growth and the pond bereft of all its summer flowers. But so it must be until another year. One important job still remains. The brick wall is now complete except for the two arches through which to enter and leave the pond. Once they are up I shall net over the water garden. This winter the fish will be safe.

Such entries as these could be the lot of any gardener. Of no significance to the world at large, they are none the worse for that. For it is through what we create or with what we live, day by day, that gives our lives most meaning. As events, thoughts and people crowd through my memory, I am aware that some of my happiest moments have been spent in the water garden. It has been an integral part of much that I have most enjoyed. On the keystone in one of the arches put up many years ago, was inscribed the saying: *'Sursum Corda'* — Lift up Your Hearts; be of Good Cheer. That is what water gardening has meant to me. And so I hope it will be for you.

Appendix I: Useful Figures and Conversions

10 mm.	=	⅜ inch
2.54 cm.	=	1 inch
30 cm.	=	12 inches
1 metre	=	3 feet 4 inches
1 sq. metre	=	10¾ sq. feet or 1.2 sq. yards
1 cubic metre	=	1.3 cubic yards
1 litre	=	1¾ pints
4.5 litres	=	1 gallon
1 kg.	=	2.2 lb.
50 kg.	=	1 cwt.

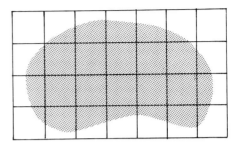

To estimate surface area of an irregular pond Divide area into squares and average out the fractions. This is a useful method of determining the amount of concrete required for the base of a pond. (The surface area is, of course, multiplied by the thickness of the concrete to give you the quantity.)

To estimate the surface area of a triangular pond It sometimes happens that a triangular pond will suit a particular part of a patio better than any other shape. This is particularly true if you have a wall meeting the patio at a sharp angle.

Surface area = ½A × B

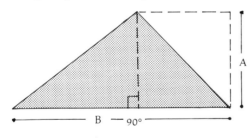

Surface area = ½A × B

To measure the surface area and circumference of a circular pond

> Area of circle = πr^2
> Circumference of circle = $2 \pi r^2$
> (π = 3.14159)

The area of the circle multiplied by the thickness of the concrete will equal the amount of concrete required for the base. The circumference of the circle multiplied by the depth of the pond, and the result multiplied by the thickness of the concrete

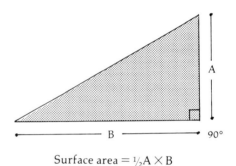

Surface area = A × C + ½A × B

will provide an estimate of the concrete required for the wall. (The estimate will be marginally on the high side.) To inscribe a circle, drive a stake into the centre of the ground. Attach to the stake a rope which should be the length of the radius of the circle. At the other end of the rope attach a sharp point (a piece of sharp wood or a heavy nail will serve the purpose). Use this to inscribe the circumference.

Polygon ponds If you want to make a regular, many-sided pond, begin by inscribing a circle whose diameter represents the maximum width of the pond. Then divide 360° by the number of sides the pond is to have. Let us say it is to be a six-sided pond. Then 360° ÷ 6 = 60°. Draw one line from the centre of the circle to the circumference i.e. one radius. Then draw a second radius at an angle of 60° to the first, then draw a third at 60° to the second and so on until six radii are drawn. (Alternatively, one could simply draw three diameters at equal intervals in this instance. This would not be possible with a seven-sided figure, for example.) Join up the six radii where they meet the circumference and the result is a hexagon. Treat as so many triangles to determine the amount of concrete required for the base.

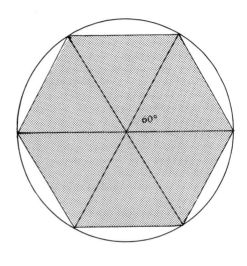

An oval pond can be made by driving two stakes into the ground and attaching a rope to them. The area inscribed by the rope will be an oval. Treat as an irregular pond to determine the surface area.

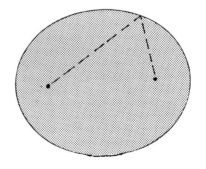

Rectangular ponds Are the dimensions of one rectangular pond more pleasing than another? The Greeks certainly thought so. Bisect one side of a square and join the mid-point to one of the opposite corners. Using this line as a radius, inscribe part of a circle to meet the extended side of the square. The resulting rectangle will have sides in the ratio 1 : 1.618; and such a rectangle is often regarded as of ideal proportions.

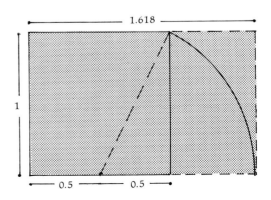

146

Appendix II: Marginal and Bog Plants

The heights of plants vary a great deal according to the conditions under which they are grown. The heights given below are those which the plant might be expected to attain under favourable conditions. DS stands for damp soil, WS for wet soil; and an entry such as DS - 6 cm. means the plant will succeed in any conditions from damp soil to 6 cm. of water over its crown.

LATIN NAME	COMMON NAME	HEIGHT	HABITAT	SEASON
Acorus calamus	Sweet Flag	60-90 cm.	WS - 5 cm.	summer
A. calamus 'Variegatus'		60-90 cm.	WS - 4 cm.	summer
A. gramineus		30 cm.	WS - 4 cm.	summer
Alisma lanceolatum	Water Plantain	30-45 cm.	WS - 20 cm.	mid-late summer
A. plantago-aquatica	Great Water Plantain	30-90 cm.	WS - 25 cm.	mid-late summer
Aruncus sylvester	Goat's Beard	1.3 m.	DS - WS	summer
A. kneiffi		60 cm.	DS - WS	summer
Astilbe arendsii		60 cm. - 1.8 m.	DS - WS	summer
A. simplicifolia		22 cm.	DS - WS	summer
Butomus umbellatus	Flowering Rush	1 m.	up to 10 cm.	summer
Calla palustris	Bog Arum	25 cm.	WS - 6 cm.	summer
Caltha palustris	King Cup, Marsh Marigold	30 cm.	WS - 6 cm.	early spring
C. palustris alba		15-20 cm.	WS - 6 cm.	early spring
C. palustris flore-pleno		25 cm.	WS - 6 cm.	early spring
C. polypetala		60-90 cm.	WS - 6 cm.	early spring
Carex pendula		1-1.3 m.	DS- WS	
C. riparia 'Bowles' Golden'		45 cm.	WS - 6 cm.	
C. stricta		1-1.3 m.	DS - WS	
Cortaderia argentea	Pampas Grass	2 m.	DS	late summer-autumn
C. quila	Pampas Grass	2 m.	DS	late summer-autumn
Cotula coronopifolia	Brass Buttons	25 cm.	WS - 6 cm.	summer
Cyperus alternifolius	Umbrella Grass	90 cm.	WS - 6 cm.	late summer
C. longus	Sweet Galingale	60 cm.-1.1 m.	DS - 6 cm.	late summer
Eriophorum angustifolium	Cotton Grass, Bog Cotton	30 cm.	WS acid	spring-early summer
E. latifolium		40 cm.	WS acid	summer
E. vaginatum		30 cm.	WS acid	summer
Filipendula ulmaria plena	Double Meadowsweet, Spirea	90cm. - 1.5cm.	DS - WS	late summer

147

Appendix

LATIN NAME	COMMON NAME	HEIGHT	HABITAT	SEASON
Glyceria aquatica variegata (*G. spectabilis*)	Manna Grass	30-90 cm.	WS - 15 cm.	summer
Gunnera manicata		2-4 m.	WS	spring
Hemerocallis	Day Lily	70 cm. - 1.2 m	DS	late summer
Hosta fortunei marginata alba	Plantain Lily	75 cm.	DS	late summer
H. glauca (sieboldiana)		60-75 cm.	DS	late summer
H. glauca fortunei (fortunei)		75 cm.	DS	late summer
H. lancifolia		60 cm.	DS	late summer
H. ventricosa		90 cm.	DS	late summer-autumn
Iris kaempferi		60-75 cm.	DS (winter) - 6 cm. (summer) acid soil	summer
I. laevigata		60 cm.	WS - 10 cm.	summer
I. pseudacorus variegatus	Yellow Flag	75 cm. - 1 m.	WS - 10 cm.	summer
I. pseudacorus bastardi		75 cm. - 1 m.	WS - 10 cm.	summer
I. sibirica		90 cm.	DS - 10 cm.	summer
I. versicolor	Blue Flag	90 cm.	WS - 10 cm.	summer
Juncus effusus spiralis	Corkscrew Rush	45 cm.	WS - 6 cm.	late summer
J. ensifolius		1m.	WS - 6 cm.	summer
Lysichitum americanum	False American Skunk Cabbage, Bog Arum	90 cm. - 1.2 m.	WS - 5 cm.	spring
L. camtschatcense		30 cm.-1 m.	WS - 6 cm.	spring
Mentha aquatica	Water Mint	30 cm.	DS - 5 cm.	late summer
Mimulus cardinalis	Monkey Flower	35 cm.	WS	summer
M. guttatus		45 cm.	WS	summer
M. luteus		45cm.	WS	summer
M. moschatus		12 cm.	WS	summer
M. ringens		50 cm.	WS - 5 cm.	summer
Myosotis scorpioides (palustris)	Water-Forget-Me-Not	20 cm.	WS - 5 cm.	summer
Orontium aquaticum	Golden Club	30-45 cm.	WS - 45 cm.	spring
Polygonum bistort	Knotwood	60 cm.	DS - WS	
Pontederia cordata	Pickerel Weed	45-75 cm.	to 12 cm.	late summer
P. lanceolata		1.5 m.	to 20 cm.	late summer

148

LATIN NAME	COMMON NAME	HEIGHT	HABITAT	SEASON
Primula beesiana		45 cm.	WS	spring
P. denticulata	Himalayan Primrose	30-45 cm.	DS	spring
P. florindae	Himalayan Cowslip	90 cm.	WS	spring
P. frondosa		15 cm.	WS	spring
P. japonica		45 cm.	WS	late spring-summer
P. pulverulenta		90 cm.	WS	summer
P. rosea		15 cm.	WS	spring
P. sikkimensis		60 cm.	WS	spring
Ranunculus aconitifolius flore-pleno	White Bachelor's Buttons Fair Maids of France	45 cm.	DS - WS	spring-early summer
R. acris flore pleno		45 cm.	DS - WS	spring-early summer
R. lingua (grandiflora)	Tongue Buttercup, Greater Spearwort	60-90 cm.	WS - 6 cm.	summer
Rheum inopinatum	Rhubarb	60 cm.	WS	late spring
R. palmatum atrosanguineum		2.5 m.	WS	late spring
Rodgersia pinnata alba		60 cm.	DS	late summer
R. pinnata elegans		60 cm.	DS	late summer
Sagittaria japonica/flore pleno	Japanese Arrowhead	75 cm.	to 15 cm.	late summer
S. sagittifolia	Common Arrowhead	50 cm.	to 15 cm.	late summer
Scirpus lacustris	Common Bulrush	1-2 m.	WS - 20 cm.	late summer
S. maritimus	Sea Club Rush	1-1.75 m.	DS - 20 cm.	late summer
S. tabernaemontani zebrinus	Porcupine Quill Rush, Zebra Rush	1.4 m.	WS - 20 cm.	late summer
Sparganium erectum	Branched Bur Reed	1 m.	to 45 cm.	late summer
Trollius europaeus	Globe Flower	45 cm.	DS - WS	summer
Typha angustifolia	Lesser Reed Mace	1-2.2 m.	WS - 60 cm.	autumn
T. latifolia	Greater Reed Mace	1.5 - 2.75 cm.	WS - 60 cm.	autumn
T. Laxmanii		75 cm. - 1.2 m.	WS - 20 cm.	autumn
T. minima		30-75 cm.	WS - 10 cm.	autumn
T. Shuttleworthii		1 - 1.3 m.	WS - 30 cm.	autumn
Veronica beccabunga	Brooklime, Speedwell	20 cm.	WS - 5 cm.	late spring-autumn
Zantedeschia aethiopica (Calla aethiopica Richardia africana)	Arum Lily	60- 90 cm.	WS - 30 cm.	summer

149

Appendix III: Ferns

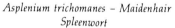

Asplenium trichomanes – Maidenhair Spleenwort

Thelypteris phegopteris – Beech Fern

Adiantum capillus veneris – True Maidenhair Fern

LATIN NAME	COMMON NAME	HEIGHT	HABITAT
Adiantum capillus veneris	True Maidenhair Fern	60 cm.	DS deep shade
A. pedatum	Hardy Maidenhair Fern	60 cm.	DS deep shade
Asplenium trichomanes	Maidenhair Spleenwort		Dry walls, partial shade
Athyrium filix-femina	Lady Fern	1 m.	WS partial or deep shade
Blechnum penna-marina		15 cm.	DS
B. spicant		70 cm.	DS
B. tabulare		45-90 cm.	WS
Dryopteris dilatata	Broad Prickly-toothed Buckler Fern	90 cm. - 1.8 m.	versatile
Matteuccia struthiopteris	Ostrich Feather Fern, Shuttlecock Fern	90 cm.	DS partial or deep shade
Onoclea sensibilis	Sensitive Fern	60 cm.	DS - WS or even shallow water, shade preferred
Osmunda regalis	Royal Fern	1.5 m.	WS
Phyllitis scolopendrium (Asplenium)	Hart's Tongue	45 cm.	DS - WS shade
Polypodium diversifolium		30 cm.	DS suited to walls
Polystichum setiferum	Soft Shield Fern	70 cm.	
Thelypteris phegopteris	Beech Fern	30 cm.	DS

Index

All marginal and bog plants described in Chapters 5 and 6 are listed in Appendix II, and ferns described in Chapter 6 are listed in Appendix III. Numbers in italics refer to illustrations.

Acorus calamus 80—1, 82
A. calamus variegatus 81, 82, 140
A. gramineus 81—2
Adiantum capillus veneris 95
A. pedatum 95
algae 13, 37—8, 119, 121, 124
Alisma lanceolatum 68
A. plantago-aquatica 67—8
American Water Thyme 38
Anchor Worms 130
aphids 125
Aponogeton distachyus 59, 60
Arum lily 68
Aruncus kneiffi 102
A. sylvester 102
Asplenium trichomanes 97
Astilbe 100, 102, 103
Athyrium filix-femina 94—5
Autumnal Starwort 40
Azolla caroliniana 42—3

Baskets 18, 38, 48, 49
Beech Ferns 95
Bitterling 110
Bladderwort 118—19
Blechnum penna-marina 96, 97
B. spicant 96
B. tabulare 96
Blue Flag 82
Bog Arum 68, 91, 139
Bog Bean 66—7, 103, 138
Bog Cotton 86, 87, 142
Brass Buttons 67
bridges 32—4
Broad Prickly-toothed Buckler Fern 96
Brooklime 69-70, 140
Brown China Marks Moth 125
Bur Reed 74—5
Butomus umbellatus 73—4
Butyl rubber liners 9, 12, 13, 35, 88

Caddis fly larvae 120, 125, 126, 141
Calla palustris 68, 139
Callitriche autumnalis 40
C. stagnalis 40, 118
Caltha palustris 65, 66
C. palustris alba 66
C. palustris flore pleno 65—6, 66
C. polypetala 66
Canadian Pondweed 39
Carassius auratus 105
Carex pendula 99
C. riparia 'Bowles' Golden' 99
C. stricta 99
catfish 111
Ceratophyllum demersum 40
C. submersum 40
Common Arrowhead 71—2
Common Water-Starwort 40

concrete cascades 28
concrete ponds 13—18
    'curing' 17
    mixture for ponds 14, 16, 123
    reinforcement 14, 16, 17, 123
constipation in fish 131
Cortaderia argentea 99
C. quila 99
cost of making a pond 34—6
Cotula coronopifolia 67, 142
cracks 13, 123
Carp, Crucian 105
    Mirror 117
Curled Pondweed 42, 118
Cyperus alternifolius 80, 81
C. longus 80

Daphnia 109, 121
Day Lily 102
depth of pond 18, 124
Ditch Moss 38
Double Meadowsweet 102
dragonfly larvae 129—30
dropsy in fish 131
Dryopteris dilatata 96
Duckweed 42, 43 121

Edging, brick 12
    concrete 12
    raised 18—19, 23
    stone 13
Eichhornia crassipes 43—4, 78
Elodea 31, 118, 134
E. canadensis 38—9, 141
E. callitrichoides 39
E. crispa 39
E. densa 39, 141
emptying a pond 18
Eriophorum 86, 87
evaporation 88, 122

Fairy Moss 42—3
False Skunk Cabbage 69
fasciation 124—5
Featherfoil 41
feeding goldfish 109, 120
ferns 94—8
fibreglass cascades 27—8
fibreglass ponds 8—9, 17, 35
Filipendula ulmaria plena 102
filtering methods 31, 32
    for aquaria 119
Flowering Rush 73—4
Fontinalis antipyretica 40
formal ponds 19, 20, 21, 22, 23, 27
fountains 30, 31, 35, 77
Frogbit 43, 111, 121, 126—7
frogs 112—13, 137
fungus diseases 124, 130

Globe Flower 102
Glyceria aquatica variegata 79, 140
Golden Club 74, 75, 139
goldfish 104, 105, 107—9, 111, 114
Golden Orfe 106, 108, 135, 136
Great Diving Beetle 128, 129
Great Water Plantain 67—8

Gudgeon 110
Gunnera manicata 99—100

Hardy Maidenhair Fern 95
Hart's Tongue 97
heaters for outdoor ponds 124
Hemerocallis 87, 102
heron 122, 127—9, 136
Hi Goi Carp 106, 107
Himalayan Cowslip 93
Hornworts 40
Hosta fortunei marginata alba 98
H. glauca 98
H. glauca fortunei 98
H. lancifolia 98
H. ventricosa 98
Hottonia palustris 41
H. inflata 41
Hydrocharis morsus-ranae 43

Ice, 13, 123, 124
informal ponds 26—7, 90
Iris 82—5, 90
I. kaempferi 84—5, 141
I. laevigata 84, 140
I. pseudacorus 82, 83, 140
I. pseudacorus bastardi 82
I. sibirica 82—3, 103, 140
I. sibirica 'Caesar' 84
I. sibirica 'Snow Queen' 84
I. variegatus 82, 125
I. versicolor 82
Ivy-leaved Duckweed 42, 121

Japanese Arrowhead 72
Juncus effusus spiralis 79—80, 125
J. ensifolius 80
Junipers 26, 135

Kingcup 65, 66
Koi Carp 104, 109

Lady Fern 94—5
Laydeker, Maurice 47
leaks 122—3, 124
leeches, fish 130
Lemna minor 42, 43
L. trisulca 42, 121
levelling the site 10, 17, 23
lice, fish 130
lights, aquarium 116
Limnaea stagnalis 111—12, 126
liner pools 9—13, 38, 50
Lotus 59—60, 62
Lysichitum americanum 69
L. camtschatcense 68—9

Maidenhair Spleenwort 97
Manna Grass 77, 143
manure 48, 49
Marsh Marigold 65, 66, 91, 134, 137, 138, 139
Matteuccia struthopteris 94
Mentha aquatica 70—1
Menyanthes trifoliata 66—7, 103
Mimulus 91—2, 143
M. cardinalis 92

151

M. guttatus 92
M. luteus 92
M. moschatus 92
M. ringens 92
minnow 110
Monkey Flowers 91, 142
Monkey Musk 92
mussels 112
Myosotis scorpioides 70, 140, 143
Myriophyllum prosperpinacoides 41
M. spicatum 41
M. verticillatum 41

Nelumbo 59—60
N. alba 'Plena' 60
N. flavescens 59—60
N. japonica 'Rubra' 60
N. 'Kermesiana' 60
N. lutea 59
N. nucifera 60, 62
N. 'Osiris' 60
N. pygmaea 'Alba' 60
netting ponds 128—9
newts 113—14, 115, 120
Nuphar advena 49
N. lutea 49
N. pumila 49
Nymphaea alba 47, 52, 53, 140
N. 'Albatross' 52
N. 'Attraction' 54
N. caerula 47, 57
N. 'Charles de Meurville' 54
N. 'Col. A. J. Walsh' 55
N. colorata 57
N. 'Colossea' 54
N. 'Conqueror' 54
N. 'Escarboucle' 53, 140, 143
N. 'Froebeli' 53, 63, 140, 143
N. 'Gloriosa' 54
N. 'Gladstoniana' 51, 52
N. 'Gloire de Temple-sur-Lot' 52
N. 'Gonnère' 52, 54
N. helvola 51
N. 'Indiana' 56
N. 'James Brydon' 54, 63, 140
N. 'Laydekeri liliacea' 55
N. 'Laydekeri Purpurata' 53, 137, 138
N. 'Marliacea Albida' 52
N. 'Marliacea Carnea' 54
N. 'Marliacea Chromatella' 55, 61, 140, 143
N. 'Marliacea Rosea' 54
N. 'Mme Wilfron Gonnère' 54
N. 'Moorei' 55, 140
N. odorata 52
N. odorata 'Sulphurea Grandiflora' 55
N. odorata 'W. B. Shaw' 55
N. 'Paul Hariot' 56
N. pygmaea alba 52, 56
N. pygmaea 'Helvola' 56
N. 'Rose Arey' 55
N. 'Sioux' 56
N. stellata 57, 62
N. 'Sunrise' 55, 56
N. tuberosa rosea 55
Nymphula nymphaeata 125

Onoclea sensibilis 94, 95
Orontium aquaticum 74, 75, 138, 139
Osmunda regalis 94
Ostrich Feather Fern 94
oxygenating plants 37—42, 111
  for aquaria 116, 118

Pampas Grass 99
Parrot's Feather 41
patio ponds 6—7, 19—26, 90
paving patterns 24, 26
paving units 23—6, 36
Perch 111
permanganate of potash 17, 130
pests, fish 127—30
  plant 125—6
Phyllitis scolopendrium 97
Pickerel weed 71, 143
Pistia stratiotes 43
plastic ponds 8—9, 35
pollution 17, 37, 109, 111, 112, 127
Polypodium diversifolium 97
Polystichum setiferum 96
polythene liners 9, 12, 13, 35
pond shapes 21, 22, 23, 124
Pontederia cordata 71, 143
pool liners 9—13, 17, 35, 123—4
  repairs to 13, 124
Pool Rush 76
Porcupine Quill Rush 77, 79
Potamogeton crispus 42, 118, 138
prefabricated ponds 8—9, 35
Primulas 92—4, 103, 139
pumps, aquarium 119
  submersible 29—31, 35
  surface 30
PVC liners 9, 12, 13, 35, 88, 123

Raised beds 26
raised ponds 23, 25, 124
Ranunculus aconitifolius flore pleno 92
R. acris flore pleno 92
R. aquatilis 241—2
R. lingua 72—3
R. lingua grandiflora 72—3
Reed Mace 76
reversion to type 125
Rheum atrosanguineum 100
R. inopinatum 100
R. palmatum 100, 101
rockery 27, 50, 96
Rodgersia pinnata alba 100, 102
R. pinnata elegans 100
roof gardens, ponds for 20, 23
Royal Fern 94

Sagittaria japonica 71—2
S. japonica flore pleno 71—2
Saprolegnia ferox 130
Scirpus lacustris 76
S. maritimus 76
S. tabernaemontani zebrinus 77, 79, 140
Sensitive Fern 94, 95
Shubunkin 106, 107
shuttering 14, 15, 16
small ponds 8, 21, 64, 88, 128

snails 111—12, 121
Soft Shield Fern 96
Sparganium erectum 74—5
Spiked Water Milfoil 41
Spirea 102
Stickleback 110—11
Stratiotes aloides 43, 44, 141
suction lift 30
Sweet Flag 80—1
Sweet Galingale 80, 134

Tape Grass 42, 118
Tench 109—10
Thelypteris phegopteris 95
Toads 113
Tongue Buttercup 72—3, 139, 140
Trapa natans 44, 78, 127
Triturus cristatus 114, 120
T. helveticus 114
T. vulgaris 113
Trollius europaeus 102
tropical water-lilies 47
True Maidenhair Fern 95
Tubifex worms 109, 120, 141
tub ponds 8
Typha angustifolia 75—6, 134, 140, 143
T. latifolia 75—6, 134, 143
T. Laxmanii 76
T. minima 143
T. Shuttleworthii 76

Umbrella Grass 80, 81

Vallisneria spiralis 42, 118
Veronica beccabunga 69—70, 142, 143
Victoria amazonica 58
Villarsia nymphoides 59, 60, 139, 141

Water-lily Aphis 125
Water Boatman 121, 128, 129, 141
Water Chestnut 43, 78, 127
Water Crowfoot 41—2, 139, 141
waterfalls and water courses 21, 27—32, 35
Water Fern 43
Water Forget-Me-Not 70, 91
Water Fringe 59, 60, 139
Water Gladiole 73, 139
Water Hawthorn 59, 60, 141
Water Hyacinth 43—4, 78, 121
Water Lettuce 44, 121
Water Mint 70—1
waterproofing concrete 14
Water Scorpion 129, 141
Water Soldier 43, 44, 121, 126—7, 141
Water Violet 41
White Bachelor's Buttons 92, 139
White Spot 130
Willow Moss 40
wrought ironwork 23, 31

Yellow Flag 82, 83

Zantedeschia aethiopica 68
Zebra Rush 77